How to Do
Self-Analysis
and Other Self-
Psychotherapies

How to Do Self-Analysis and Other Self-Psychotherapies

Louis A. Gottschalk, M.D.

JASON ARONSON INC.
Northvale, New Jersey
London

The author gratefully acknowledges permission to reprint excerpts from the article on pp. 109–116, from: Deane H. Shapiro, Jr., and Roger N. Walsh (Eds.), Meditation: Classic and Contemporary Perspectives. New York: Aldine de Gruyter. Copyright © 1984 by Deane H. Shapiro, Jr. and Roger N. Walsh.

Library of Congress Cataloging-in-Publication Data

Gottschalk, Louis A.
    How to do self-analysis and other self-psychotherapies / by Louis
A. Gottschalk.
      p.   cm.
    Bibliography: p.
    Includes index.
    ISBN 0-87668-847-4
    1. Psychotherapy—Popular works.   2. Self-care, Health.
I. Title.
RC480.5.G648   1989
616.89'14—dc19
                                   89-30781
                                   CIP

Manufactured in the United States of America. Jason Aronson Inc. offers books and cassettes. For information and catalog write to Jason Aronson Inc., 230 Livingston Street, Northvale, New Jersey 07647.

To the memory of my daughter
Susan Elizabeth Gottschalk-Smith
and in gratitude for the help and devotion of my wife,
Helen Clarissa Reller Gottschalk, M.D.

Contents

Preface

A book on self-analysis and other kinds of self-psychotherapy, written by someone who has for over four decades been an educator of professional social workers, psychologists, psychiatrists, and psychoanalysts, needs an explanation. Why would an adherent of the highest standards of each of these disciplines write a book for lay readers about how they might gain some of the knowledge and skills acquired by professionals only after many years of formal education and personal supervision?

I do not believe that this or any other similar book can supplant the expertise achieved through accredited graduate programs. My aims here are more modest.

First, this book attempts to take the mystery out of the process of psychotherapy, and invites the reader to try out some of these procedures to become familiar with how they feel and how they may change ways of thinking, feeling, and behaving. Some individuals will discover that they have a surprising aptitude for the use of one or more of these procedures. Others will find that none works for them. These differences may result from individual variations in the degree of psychological-mindedness or in the nature of the mental problems needing help. Some problems require the immediate help of one or several other people, and it is important to recognize this early and to act on it. On the other hand, many of life's problems can initially be tackled by self-reflection and self-scrutiny; afterwards, in such cases, a professionally trained expert is required to help with or complete the task. Furthermore, many people cannot afford professional help for mental problems, or do not find such help to be readily accessible or available in their vicinity. Hence, there is a need for self-help guidelines that might suffice until conditions change to enable the needy individual to pay for the help of a professional. Or perhaps the self-help procedures may be adequate to carry the individual over a rough spot or crisis until the emotional problem has run its natural course.

You might wonder whether there could be harmful effects from trying to do such a job by yourself. I do not think there are any, for these are the same procedures that are recommended for and used by professionally trained persons. You might ask if there is not a danger that matters might get worse if you tried to fix them yourself, just as if you tried to repair your own auto, television, or plumbing. The answer is no. You are much more familiar with your self and how you feel and think than you are with the workings of a mechanical or electrical machine or a plumbing fixture. The worst that could happen if you try some kind of self-help procedure described here is that you might get little or no relief for your discomfort or emotional conflict. If that should occur, you ought to seriously consider consulting an expert — maybe, first, your family doctor or your clergyman or someone else whom you consider reliable, trustworthy, and knowledgeable about such matters.

I suggest that you consider this book something like a family almanac, giving you information about how intelligent, informed, and well-trained individuals view psychoanalysis and various other kinds of psycho-therapy, including meditation and religion. You will learn about the possible applications of these to your self and on your own, and about the limitations of such applications. Trying out some of these methods can be an enlightening experience.

1

Introduction

The terms "self-analysis" and "self-psychotherapy" cover a wide range of procedures and phenomena. Some limits need to be set in order to focus on an understandable and well-defined theme.

Self-analysis and self-psychotherapy refer to those self-help procedures designed to increase your comprehension and knowledge about yourself in order to improve the quality of your life and to help you cope with the problems of human existence. Since there are many different methods of learning about yourself, it may be helpful to classify these into categories, even though these methods and goals often share certain overlapping features.

DIFFERENT METHODS

"Self-Psychoanalytic" Procedures

Self-analysis, based on psychoanalytic principles, has been encouraged and taught by psychoanalysts. In fact, most psychoanalysts recommend that the patient develop the ability to carry out self-analysis through continual self-scrutiny, using free association and dream analysis. Sigmund Freud himself provided the model for this process. He conducted his own psychoanalysis, supervised occasionally through his correspondence with his friend, Wilhelm Fliess, with whom he shared his self-discoveries. Continuing self-analysis and self-scrutiny is also recommended by psychiatrists and other clinicians who obtain training and education in psychoanalysis.

In 1942 Karen Horney wrote *Self-Analysis* to light the way for others to follow. Moreover, a rich body of psychoanalytic literature has evolved on the subject of countertransference (Renik 1986), which is a psychotherapist's biased reactions to a patient, the awareness of which requires psychoanalytic self-analysis. This self-analysis is encouraged by most training programs. The student is involved in improving his or her psychotherapeutic skills and in developing an enhanced capacity for self-awareness, in order to avoid possible pitfalls in the psychotherapy of others.

Other Self-Psychotherapies

Other self-psychotherapies have been developed that do not rely heavily on psychoanalytic theory and practice.

These methods are varied, and are described in more detail later. They merit consideration here because they too aim to increase self-awareness and reduce symptomatic distress. These self-psychotherapies include behavior and conditioning therapy, autogenic training, self-hypnosis, and a very questionable procedure known as "crystal healing." Meditation and religious practices are also included here, for these activities seek to soothe and heal the woes of living through mental processes.

Meditation

The term *meditation* refers to a collection of practices that train one's attention in order to heighten awareness and bring mental processes under greater voluntary control. The ultimate aims of these practices are the development of insight into the nature of reality and of one's own mental processes, consciousness, and identity, and the development of optimal states of psychological well-being and consciousness. However, meditation can also be used for a variety of intermediate aims, such as psychotherapeutic and psychophysiological benefits (Walsh 1983).

Religious Self-Scrutiny

Many religions have fostered religious self-examination and criticism. This may be achieved through solitary retreats lasting from a few hours to many months, during which the person's relationship to a deity and to existence are explored through various methods aimed to increase self-awareness. This category of religious self-analysis is elaborated upon later in this book.

CHOOSING A PSYCHOTHERAPY

Diverse Approaches: Western versus Eastern Psychological Models

In the Western world there is increasing interest in Eastern psychology and meditative practice. It is probably fair to say that as Pacific rim countries become more and more involved in trade and economic rivalry with the Western world, Western ways of thinking and feeling are also pervading these Eastern cultures. The end result of these current broad intercommunications between Western and Eastern cultures will eventually result in their becoming more similar.

It has become a vogue among a certain group of pioneers spirits in the Western world to adopt, with a missionary zeal, some Eastern psychologies—thereby emphasizing an adversarial approach in the comparison of Eastern and Western practices. Western proponents of Eastern psychologies set the levels of discussion and argument around states of consciousness and the values of meditative practices. The normal or usual state of consciousness, experienced when one is free of the influence of intoxicating chemicals or the consequences of physical disease or mental disorder, is regarded as a *lower* state of consciousness. The states of consciousness achievable through meditative practices are viewed to be on a higher level. From the perspective of one meditative model our usually normal state of consciousness is "suboptimal, out of control and gives us only a distorted perception of reality while failing to recognize this distortion" (Walsh 1983). From this meditative perspective, our usual state of consciousness is seen as a hypnotically constricted trance. The continual sensory messages from our five senses — seeing, hearing, smelling, tasting, and touching — are considered illusory, merely registrations of the external environment via our physical sensory organs. Moreover, the continuing recurrences of memory images from our brain that enter into our consciousness are regarded as noise in what could otherwise be a harmonious musical phenomenon. The fact that many different levels of consciousness can be achieved through meditation is held forth as evidence of the superiority of Eastern psychologies in understanding the mind.

Western psychologies focus on handling and coping with reality problems by trying to overcome them. If this is not possible, these psychologies strive toward understanding the effects of life events on the self throughout life, in order to improve and update the coping mechanisms one employs in dealing with reality. The ecstatic states sometimes achievable through meditation are viewed as worthwhile temporary experiences transiently reproducing the ego states that one may have experienced while pleasantly receiving nutrition from the mother's breast or enjoying the relatively quiescent intrauterine existence. That the recall and experiencing of any such state might make a person capable of dealing with a contemporary real-life problem, or provide an appropriate means of solving some interpersonal discord or some vocational obstacle, would be regarded as unlikely. On the other hand, the capacity to recall or otherwise engender states of bliss or human harmony and love is seen as a useful catalyst toward increasing one's hope that the problem being faced in reality can, eventually, be mastered.

To summarize, I would conclude that the major differences between Western and Eastern psychological approaches are based upon the fact that Western psychologies generally deal with the products of normal thinking and feeling as useful methods of coping with a challenging but sometimes harsh and painful world. In addition, Western psychologies tend to hold that the transitory mental images and memories continually conjured up by our brains are not random disorders but flashbacks of different self-states brought back to awareness when we are faced with new coping experiences. On the other hand, Eastern psychologies hold that these memory flashbacks are meaningless and disharmonious, and that the best way to cope with reality problems is through periodic escape and withdrawal into private meditative sessions in which one works toward suppressing the continual input and interplay of recurring memories. For Eastern psychologies the capacity to achieve a transient state of peace (*nirvana*) provides a welcome retreat from the frustrations and sufferings of reality. The capacity to control and bring on such transient psychological states, it is argued, can give one a sense of understanding and control of one's self as well as a sense of being part of the universe. After such a meditative high, one can supposedly return to external reality with, perhaps, a renewed energy to cope with problems — and a feeling of self-assurance that one still has oneself and the capacity to reevoke pleasant conscious states without pain and with blurred memories of external travail.

Since these somewhat contrary approaches have both been useful to countless millions of people in helping them to understand and cope with the pleasures or pains of life, conceivably both must have some benefits. It is hard to believe, in fact, that there is simply one cure-all approach to dealing with the problems of living and existing. Rather, one approach may be better in dealing with some life problems, whereas another approach may be better in dealing with others. This viewpoint, in any event, is the one being supported in this book.

Personal Preferences and Aptitudes

In considering which kind of self-psychotherapy to select, one must consider several relevant factors. The first is your preference and your degree of expertise in using one method over another.

When a psychotherapist or counselor is sought, the presumption is that this person has had professional training in a number of different types of psychotherapy, and has achieved both proficiency and credentials in the techniques. Undertaking the responsibility to do an expert's task yourself requires some recognition that, without appropriate training, we are not all equally gifted or experienced. This book has guidelines for do-it-yourselfers that summarize how experts with different approaches are trained. It aims to encourage some readers, especially those who do not have access to such experts or who are interested in improving their own skills toward self-understanding, to make some progress in the area of self-help. Thus, to begin with, you should consider your aptitudes and preferences, and on the basis of these choose one of the broad types of techniques (or any combination of them) as a first step. Since different life problems and goals can influence your decision about which technique to employ, and since different techniques are more likely to be successful with certain problems than others, a review of such problem areas and possible goals should be carried out. Also, your overall goal — whether you are seeking temporary relief from a problem, or a major change in your personality traits — certainly makes a difference with respect to which kind of psychotherapy to undertake. This is as true when you are seeking professional psychotherapeutic help from someone else as it is when you are trying to train yourself to be your own psychotherapist.

Matching the Psychotherapy to the Problem

Let us consider here some of the different areas in which you might like to effect some improvement in the quality of your life. Then, in a following section, we consider several time factors which might influence the type of psychotherapeutic approach you choose.

Interpersonal and Social Problems

In the event that one's goal is to remedy certain interpersonal and social problems, there is likely to be more success through using one of the Western psychological approaches than one of the Eastern types. Eastern meditative approaches help one to familiarize oneself with different levels of one's own consciousness; such enlightenment—although offering temporary relief from the strains and stresses of interpersonal problems—is not likely to lead to insight concerning a person's own adverse contributions to these problems. On the other hand, the Western approaches, especially those that focus on mutually productive and unproductive behaviors, are more likely to focus on techniques that may lead to improvement in interpersonal relationships. Generalizations such as "It takes two to tango," or "There are two sides to every argument" contain some common wisdom that obliges the individual to examine not only how much blame can be placed on others, but also how much responsibility one must place on one's own self. As in most social or political conflicts, compromise can result if each individual cooperates in the conflict resolution. Moreover, you must question yourself about whether you are characteristically subject to similar interpersonal and social difficulties with others. You may be involved in long-standing problems that need some kind of continuous and long-term psychotherapy.

Meditative and religious self-scrutiny may, for some individuals, provide the strength or motivation to solve or try to solve these interpersonal problems, especially if they are recurring ones. In my experience, however, these approaches seem to have a minimal effect on increasing one's altruism or promoting strenuous efforts to change one's social behavior. They seem to encourage withdrawal from the interpersonal situation, or grudging tolerance of the other person; the latter may work out at least in terms of preserving the relationship. Meditative and religious self-scrutiny can have definite effects on your existential views — that is, views about your place and purpose in the universe. New decisions about such existential issues may influence how you perceive and behave in interpersonal and social situations.

Domestic Problems

What has been said regarding interpersonal and social situations also applies directly to domestic problems. However, moral and legal interpersonal commitments add more complicated aspects to these problems. In addition, the presence of children can broaden and deepen the scope of a couple's problems.

There are many mental health professionals who claim proficiency in dealing with domestic problems. These range from psychoanalysts, psychiatrists, and psychologists to marital counselors without advanced degrees and to pastoral counselors. Many engage both spouses in the enterprise of resolving problems. Marital therapy, as well as psychotherapy with one spouse, often is of considerable help.

Can self-analysis or self-psychotherapy, in the face of the complexity of such problems, offer any help? The answer is probably yes. Self-analysis, self-psychotherapy, and religious or meditative self-scrutiny all seem able to help bring about turning points in dysfunctional marriages.

Vocational and Occupational Problems

One must consider whether vocational and occupational problems are minor and temporary, or major problems with long-standing implications. The escape or withdrawal route does not, at first glance, seem practical or effective, whether the difficulties stem primarily from within the work situation itself or from within the individual. For short-term and minor problems, meditative and religious self-scrutiny may provide some relief until the storm blows over. When short-term psychotherapeutic approaches are clung to in situations that involve long-standing problems, additional avoidance techniques are likely to be employed; examples are alcoholism or chemical substance abuse, or the transformation of a vocational or occupational problem into a social or domestic one.

Problems of Performers and Athletes

Some individuals devote their lives to providing recreation for others through the entertainment industry or through sports. The kinds of problems these individuals face are different from those encountered by individuals in more private areas of endeavor. Problems facing a movie actress whose beauty is fading or a professional athlete whose physical prowess is weakening may be helped by any one of the self-psychotherapy approaches, depending on the specific problem. In the course of taking part in the performing arts or professional sports, it is almost impossible to employ meditative or religious self-scrutiny because it is necessary to be so involved in the external world. Various psychological devices have been successfully used by sports professionals to coach themselves into a winning posture or position, and some of these are described later.

Existential Problems

At first consideratiom, meditative and religious approaches would seem to be the best techniques in trying to establish one's identity and to clarify one's belief system with respect to the purpose of existence. This notion is, indeed, valid. But various neurotic or irrational distortions, often stemming from early childhood, can influence one's existential views so that they are extraordinarily pessimistic or narissistic. Here a Western approach to self-psychotherapy is necessary to bring about long-lasting changes.

Interpersonal Problems

How you feel and perceive your self and the different selves experienced over your lifetime is the focus of long-term individual psychotherapy of the Western type, combined with continuing self-analysis. Proponents of Eastern psychology claim that they obtain considerable self-understanding through focusing on their own levels of consciousness, while inhibiting the ripples and reflections of their own free associations and recurring memories. This indicates that maybe the meditative and mystical approaches are worth a try. Religious self-scrutiny, which is focused on maintaining your relationship to a supreme deity, can influence your attitude toward your own personal needs and urges. Hence, religious self-scrutiny, for some individuals, is essential for maintaining a delicate balance between secular, earthly needs and spiritual ones.

Goals and the Time Involved in Psychotherapy

The type of self-psychotherapy that one might select is not only influenced by the issues just discussed, but also by the degree of change one wants and anticipates. A relatively minor personality quirk or emotional reaction is certainly likely to require less reeducation, and therefore less psychotherapy, than a complete overhaul of the personality. When a professional expert is engaged to facilitate personality changes or deal with a life problem, such professionals adapt their techniques and procedures to fit a range of goals. It is difficult to pinpoint which of the different kinds of psychotherapy, or combinations of these, might be most effective toward reaching minor or major psychotherapeutic goals. However, some generalizations can be made.

Short-Term Goals

For those personality problems or emotional reactions requiring a relatively short time to remedy, meditative techniques and religious approaches are adequate. For example, in the case of a mild anxiety attack or a depressive mood, meditative approaches can provide quick, though often temporary, relief. For religious devotees, the ritual of participating in the confessional offers relief for feelings associated with sin. A religious service providing reassurances that one will be reunited with a deceased loved one can facilitate feelings of peace and equanimity that no other psychotherapy can readily match. Likewise, self-initiated meditative and/or religious procedures can be equally effective in helping cope with such goals. Psychodynamic or psychoanalytically oriented psychotherapies are also, for the person who has developed some personal skills in these methods, capable of relieving troublesome short-term symptoms and emotional distress. There are many individuals who do not have strong religious beliefs or faith, and for these persons nonreligious types of psychotherapy can be appropriately effective for short-term goals.

Long-Term Goals

Major personality changes, and recovery from extremely stressful life experiences, take time and cannot be accomplished easily, if at all. Western psychotherapies were designed to try to achieve such change by seeking out the original and contributing causes of problems — and, after so doing, by evolving better ways of viewing, understanding, and coping with these causes and the adverse habits that result. Self-psychoanalysis and self-psychotherapy, for individuals who have developed some skills in these approaches, can be quite effective toward reaching such long-term goals.

The Eastern psychological approach is more concerned with a turning away from so-called materialistic goals. Buddhism, Hinduism, and other Eastern religions have been effective in helping countless generations cope with subjugation, tyranny, poverty, and pestilence, and they are still capable of doing so.

Christianity and Judaism have also provided existential ways of dealing with the problems of existence. Thus, religious conversion is another possible means of achieving long-term goals. The ways in which such long-term goals are approached are obviously quite different from each other, as are their end results. In an enlightened, tolerant, and unbiased society it would be inappropriate to say one outcome or result is better than another, for such an evaluative conclusion depends on the criteria one selects for drawing such conclusions.

Future, Present, or Past Problems

The problems one wants to deal with may have occurred in the past, may be occurring in the present, or may be something one has to face in the future. Not all psychotherapies are equally suited to deal with all these time factors.

Future Problems   Suppose one is focusing on future events — for example, on enhancing one's performance in the future, or on achieving the prevention of future interpersonal problems. Such goals require procedures that are related to the world as it is, and preoccupations with one's psychology and behavior as they are in that world. Therefore, religious approaches — such as prayer or improving one's relationship with a supreme being, or studying the various levels of consciousness one can bring about — will not provide all the help that is necessary toward achieving future goals. The major exception to this statement is that the meditative or religious approaches may help to maintain one's motivation and incentive to learn the skills and adaptive mechanisms needed to reach such future goals.

Current Problems   Again, in dealing with current problems, both the direct approach of the Western psychologies and the indirect approach of the Eastern psychologies (that is, temporarily retreating before one returns to the fray) have merits. Whether the current problem involves major or minor adjustments of one's behavior or one's emotional reactions, the degree of adjustment needed will play a part in the psychotherapeutic procedure selected.

Past Problems   Focus on the past could involve discovering the origins of one's present behavior; whereas a preoccupation with the past could involve the unwanted recurrence of intrusive thoughts and emotions concerning past events. To understand the early origins of one's psychological and behavioral reactions, psychodynamic and psychoanalytic therapies are most appropriate. With intrusive thoughts originating from past events or with flashbacks of painful ego states—for example, irrepressible memories originating with physical torture or child abuse—the detailed recovery and understanding of these events, and relief from their consequences, require some form of psychodynamic or psychoanalytic therapy. The extent to which the meditative or religious psychotherapy approaches can remedy these kinds of problems, on a permanent rather than a short-term basis, has not been explored; or, if it has been explored, the results have not been widely reported.

HISTORICAL BACKGROUND

Pre-Freud

Before Sigmund Freud there were countless methods used to try to change human behavior and bring about peace of mind. How to relieve human distress, to attain new achievements, to best enjoy the pleasures of life, have always been subjects of human inquiry. Guidelines on how to achieve personal equanimity, to be at peace with a God or the gods, and on the meaning of man in the Universe, have been the subjects of philosophy, ethics, drama, and literature. Human warfare has been employed for such purposes and has always been rationalized as the only means of accomplishing certain secular or religious beliefs. The history of human thought and exploring ways of influencing it has evolved through the Africans, the Egyptians, the Greeks, the Europeans, and the Asians. Tracing and discussing these details would be a task far beyond the scope of this little book. Freud's endeavors were certainly influenced by countless predecessors. He gave credit to some of them, but to most he did not.

Freud

Sigmund Freud (1856–1939) is notable, among other things, for his work on self-psychoanalysis and self-psychotherapy. He preoccupied himself with such endeavors and then, being such a prolific and hardworking writer, he wrote so well about them that he attracted many students. His inquiring, intelligent, and innovative mind has stimulated generations up to the present time to try to explore their unconscious minds and the infantile and childhood origins of their adult psychology. Freud's self-analysis provides a model for us of the usefulness of free association, and of attention to one's seemingly irrelevant and peripheral thoughts and feelings to help recall forgotten experiences and memories — that is, to make the unconscious conscious.

Freud demonstrated in his own self-analysis that the welter of thoughts and feelings generated by our brains are indeed the markers of the variety of past experiences and memories that we have lived through. Every one of these thoughts has an origin in our past sensory and cognitive experiences. An especially innovative contribution of Freud's were his insights into the process of dreaming and his discoveries that dreams were a potential royal road to the unconscious. He came to recognize that there are three major psychological mechanisms in the process of dreaming: symbolization, condensation, and displacement. These psychological mechanisms are defined and explained later.

Pavlov

Ivan Petrovich Pavlov (1849–1936) is credited with giving conditioned reflexes their name. His influence on learning theory has been considerable. Learning theory concerns us to some extent in this book when the possibilities of learning and self-re-education are discussed. Moreover, behavior and conditioning therapy, which can be administered as a self-psychotherapy, explicitly stems from the learning theory model. Pavlov's classical conditioning experiment is familiar: when meat powder is placed in a dog's mouth, salivation takes place. The food is called the *unconditioned stimulus* and the salivation the *unconditioned response*. When an additional stimulus, such as a light, is combined with the presentation of food, the light will eventually — after repetition — evoke salivation. The light is termed the *conditioned stimulus* and the response to it the *conditioned reflex* or *conditioned response*. Though we by no means deal in detail or directly with the complex aspects of learning theories in this book, it is important to stress that one's own consciously initiated thoughts, emotions, and actions, as well as the behavior of others, can be associated in one's mind with rewards or punishments that reinforce feelings and behaviors. There are many principles of learning that form a scientific background and basis for the phenomena discussed in these pages.

2

Beginning Psychotherapy

In order to select the best method of psychotherapy for yourself, it is first advisable to articulate and communicate to yourself the nature of your problem. Let us list and classify some possibilities.

CLASSIFYING THE PROBLEM AREA

Subjective and Intrapersonal Problems

The problem might fall into any classification and may seem to be characterized by symptoms such as anxiety, hostility, or depression. Often it may not be possible to pinpoint the source of these subjective feelings. You may have only a slight idea as to what might be triggering them. Then you need to decide whether your problem is primarily subjective, rather than the result of an experience or event produced by something in your environment.

Social and Interpersonal Problems

Symptoms may be recognized as a result of some social situation, an interpersonal relationship with one individual or several. Or the problem might seem to be occurring when you simply think about or anticipate being involved with another person or persons.

Domestic Problems

The situation and context could be similar to the social and interpersonal one, but involve primarily your spouse or children. Or the problem could involve other significant people in your life such as your parents, grandparents, aunts, or uncles.

Vocational and Occupational Problems

The problem might involve social relations taking place primarily at the workplace, or involve your vocation or occupation. The termination of a job is associated with distress and some other uncomfortable feelings and consequences.

Economic Problems

Your problem may not seem to fall into any of the above categories; rather, it might be primarily associated with your economic situation. Money and finances can certainly influence how one feels about oneself, and can thus affect one's sense of well-being. A minimum income is required to take care of one's needs for food, clothing, shelter, and physical health. At the other extreme, for some people, the drive to acquire large amounts of money, or the experience of obtaining and managing such funds, may precipitate stress.

Existential Problems

Everyone develops some belief concerning the meaning of existence and the possibility of life after death. Individuals may change these beliefs, be in the process of formulating them, or become more preoccupied with such issues than they previously were. Continual preoccupation with and worries about such matters, including pressing questions about your own identity, are existential problems.

It is not uncommon for people to find that their problems seem to involve several classifications. The preceding descriptions may help you decide what kind of self-psychotherapy might be most effective in dealing with your particular problems.

CONSIDERING VARIOUS TEMPORAL ISSUES

Various aspects of your problem may involve different time periods in your life, and this fact may influence the type of self-psychotherapy you might choose to help yourself. As was previously indicated, some kinds of problems require only short-term self-psychotherapy; other problems require more time. And some problems involve difficulties that occurred in the past, whereas others involve those occurring in the present; still other problems are based upon what will have to be faced in the future. In trying to select which type of self-psychotherapy might be most useful, you have to do exactly what a professional psychotherapist is obliged to do and that is to try to determine these temporal issues. It is a good idea to jot down which of these variables you want to focus on.

DECIDING THE SCOPE
OF THE PSYCHOTHERAPY

Focal

You may want to focus on one aspect of your personality, whether large or small, or only on a specific problem and goal. In this instance, you could consider that the scope of the psychotherapy you want to pursue is a focal and specific goal involving yourself.

Global

It may well be that you are dissatisfied with a major aspect of your personality and want to undergo and achieve considerable remodeling. In this instance, the goals of your psychotherapy are global; that is, they involve seeking changes in a large portion of yourself and your personality.

GETTING UNDERWAY

Listing Your Goals
and Other Important Factors

To get underway, it is a good idea to write down your goals and other benefits that you seek to achieve through your self-psychotherapy. After doing so, go back over the preceding pages in order to try to classify the characteristics of the personal problems for which you want some help. This will help guide you toward selecting the type of self-psychotherapy that is most likely to be appropriate and successful.

Selecting the Method

You should now have done enough thinking and planning to help you decide what method of self-psychotherapy you want to select. Guidelines for the different methods of psychotherapy follow.

3

The Psychoanalytic

Approach

In previous sections there were some guidelines suggesting the kinds of problems and goals for which the psychoanalytic approach is better suited than other types of psychotherapy.

If you intend to use the psychoanalytic method, it helps to try to set aside fifteen to forty-five minutes a day for several days a week. The psychoanalytic method encourages the use of free association, introspection, dream analysis, and continuing self-scrutiny. Free association and dream analysis are used in order to discover those unconscious memories or forgotten experiences that may be influencing the problematic feelings or behavior you are trying to understand. The person using the psychoanalytic approach should, first, sit in a comfortable chair or lie on a couch in a quiet room.

During the process of psychoanalysis, the patient experiences attitudes and feelings toward the therapist that are similar to those experienced with important people during childhood or other periods of development. The clarification and verbalizing of these thoughts and feelings to the psychoanalyst distinguish psychoanalytic therapy from other types of psychotherapy. The therapist, too, is inclined to relive and experience many highly emotional reactions toward the patient and toward the information the patient shares. These are called countertransference reactions. Customarily, a good psychoanalyst carefully observes his or her reactions in order to discriminate those which may hinder or distort responses to the patient; this would be the case with reactions that are peculiar or unique to the therapist and not to the patient's life experiences. Or these reactions of the therapist may in some other way bias his or her therapeutic efforts. It will be important later in this discourse to explain how a person doing self-analysis can effectively keep an eye on both the portion of the self seeking therapy (that is the patient) and the portion of the self functioning as the therapist (that is, the psychoanalyst). No other type of psychotherapy concentrates so much on the interface and possible conflicts between these two poles of the psychotherapeutic situation and process.

FREE ASSOCIATION

The first major method of self analysis is free-association. The process of free association involves

letting yourself experience any thoughts and feelings
that might be related — whether closely or vaguely — to
the initial thoughts and feelings you have been experiencing. An effort needs to be made to inhibit or quiet
the usual censorship you exercise in guiding and exe-
cuting your thinking. Rather, it is appropriate to allow
any marginal or peripheral thoughts or feelings that
might seem unrelated to seep into your stream of
consciousness. These stray emotions and thoughts are
often regarded as more important and revealing than
the obviously coherent and connected mental processes.
The reason for this viewpoint is that these less coherent,
seemingly unrelated mental processes and ideas help
reveal subconscious feelings and attitudes involved in
the subject matter you are surveying.

The process is something like panning for gold,
when much of the material you are examining can be
thrown away and only small bits and pieces of the
material you are examining constitute valuable nug-
gets. Obviously, the process of free association requires
continuing introspection and subjective self-scrutiny.
For some people this is easy and natural. For others,
who are inhibited, this is a process that takes some time
to get used to carrying out. The general goal is to try to
recall and to clarify all the details you can about the
times and episodes in which you experienced the
conflict or problem you are trying to understand. It is
quite appropriate to try to recollect the earliest time in
your life when the personal problem was encountered.
As these details and this subjective adventure go on, an
attempt should be made to try to follow honestly all the
branches of your thought processes that might be
inviting themselves to be explored, even if they appear
to be only vaguely related to the initial steps taken in

thinking about some detail of the problem which you want to understand better.

After a period of this self-reflection, it often helps to write in summary fashion what actually occurred during this process of free association. It does not matter if no obvious insights are achieved immediately or even for weeks thereafter. Some individuals may, however, make some important self-discoveries early in this process.

The overall goal in starting out is to try to describe to yourself a full story-line of all that you can remember about when the problem was first recognized, how it began to manifest itself, under what circumstances it occurred and recurred, which people were principally involved when the problem first showed up, and so forth. You will be searching for connections between various events that were previously not recognized. All of us may dissociate and/or fail to see the connections between events and experiences that have significant emotional interrelationships.

It is useful to briefly read over the notes from one or several of the preceding self-psychoanalytic sessions, before starting the next session. This helps keep you on track so that you can proceed to the next chapter of your self-analysis. Periodically reading your notes thoroughly and in depth can indicate if and when you have begun to go astray in avoiding some areas that were important but too disturbing to pursue. This is discussed later in the section on the middle phases of self analysis.

In continuing the process of free association, you need to get into a relaxed state of mind; after so doing, you should first focus on the total emotional conflict or the overall behavior problem you want to learn more about, or any particular aspect of this problem. Then you can quietly observe the first thoughts or mental images, whether they be visual, auditory, or some other sensory modality, of which you might be reminded from this starting point. At this juncture, the free-association process will continue if you do not purposely think about another topic to block out the flow of thoughts moving along with the stream of consciousness. You can let these thoughts, emotions, and sensory images flow along for a period of five minutes or more. Periodically, it is helpful to interrupt the flow of these free associations to ask yourself what they have told you about the original subject. During these usually brief interruptions you are asking another part of your mind to survey the words, mental images, and sensory experiences that occurred during the preceding period of free association. You are now trying to formulate what was learned during the free-associative process. The mental attitude you now try to evoke requires a different intellectual and critical perspective than your more relaxed, uncritical, free-thinking, passive position during the process of free association.

These periods of brief surveying and assessing the products of free association can give you a more precise idea than you previously had of the mental or emotional connections between psychopathological conflicts and deviant behavior. The connections might be of a psychodynamic nature — that is, they might provide some understanding of what the psychological relationship is between one event or experience and another mental or emotional event; or they may give you an idea about the psychosocial or biomedical origins of the initial problem. Sometimes this kind of information is referred to as a "psychogenetic" perspective, referring to hypotheses that provide information about sources or factors contributing to the origins of the problem areas. Such information may be enlightening with respect to some specific aspect of the abnormal behavior; in such an instance it is often referred to as a "focal" or recent origin of the emotional conflict. The earliest roots of the abnormal behavior or conflict are sometimes referred to as the "nuclear" origins.

To carry out the process of free association, you do not need to have any prior conception of how to organize and make use of the data obtained. Freud started out using this free-associative process without clear concepts about what he was going to discover. He made steady headway in using free association toward the goal of understanding himself and various aspects of his childhood neurosis. With the help of several generations of other experienced psychoanalysts, he developed a good understanding of the origins and structure of psychoneurosis and other personality disorders. Fortunately, the person using the free-associative process today to search his or her mind does not have to spend years trying to organize the best way to assemble all the available data, in order to comprehend why some form of neurosis, personality disorder, or more severe type of mental disorder has evolved.

There are many good books describing the psychoanalytic viewpoints about mental disorders. Though additional literature is not necessary, the following readings are recommended as supplements to the present book: Horney (1942), Freud (1949), Alexander and Ross (1952), Gottschalk (1985).

PSYCHOANALYTIC VIEWS
ON THE NATURE
OF EMOTIONAL DISORDERS

Modern psychoanalysis teaches that there are genetic and hereditary factors that lay down the basis for the diverse potentialities that we develop. These inherited characteristics can be modified by physical and chemical, as well as biological, events. In addition, there are various ways in which psychological and social experiences can further mold and shape the stuff of which we are made.

During our intrauterine life we are certainly exposed to physical and biochemical events that may hamper or facilitate growth and development. The effects of psychosocial stimuli on the developing fetus are limited. However, once we have come through the birth canal and filled our lungs with air, we are subject to an increasing number of interactions with others. Parents, grandparents, hired people, all react to the infant differently. The same will be true throughout childhood. Moreover, the environment into which a child is born varies for all of us. For example, there may be no children in a family or a number of them, a biological mother or two biological parents or none, adoptive parents or many different kinds of caretakers. The geographical location and climate, the child's nutrition, and the cultural milieu will vary considerably. The amount and quality of loving and tender care, and any exposure to aggression and violence, are also variables.

The psychoanalytic viewpoint is that these early life experiences, from earliest infancy and throughout childhood, provide continual learning experiences that become biologically imprinted on the child's nervous system. The earlier the stressful life experiences, the more widespread and ingrained the effect may be. This idea is expressed in the metaphor, "As the twig is bent so grows the tree."

As we grow and develop in childhood each one of us does the best he or she can in dealing with frustrations and hardships, and, in the process of so doing, each one of us develops new and better ways of coping with stressful life experiences. And these different coping mechanisms become part of our regular and habitual way of existing, living, and achieving what is expected of us in the different corners of the world in which we live.

Because we are such helpless and unprotected mammals when we come into the world, we require considerable long-term nurturing and educating. Our self-concept in early infancy, if we are sufficiently wanted and loved, becomes one of high self-worth and allows feelings of potential magical powers — for an unintelligible cry is likely to bring food, a grunt is likely to call forth another kind of attention, and a smile may bring the brush of another person's cheeks or lips against ours. From this relative paradise in infancy (a state of "primary narcissism"), we acquire a self-concept of grandeur and omnipotence. In early childhood we find ourselves having to prove our worth through demonstrating various performances and achieving goals set by others (a state of "secondary narcissism"). Any expectations by those in our environment that we demonstrate achievements before we are mature and developed enough to do so may lead to psychological injuries to our self-esteem. Likewise, our inability as little children to comply with unreasonable expectations by parental figures may leave continuing memories of vague incompetence. On the other hand, wholesale adoration by one or several members of a large family may lead us to have a child's sense of being a superman or superwoman with entitlements of the highest royalty. In contrast, the witnessing of sad or tragic events during childhood may leave marks on us that cannot be easily erased.

Psychoanalysis teaches that during our early growth and development we pass through a number of stages and, hence, we are conscious of different identities or different selves during these stages of development. Our repertoire of how to cope or deal with frustrating life experiences tends to grow and become more sophisticated, as our understanding of the world and how it works increases. All of us are susceptible to developing an infantile or childhood neurosis, because we are likely to fall back and use self-concepts and coping mechanisms that were more appropriate to an earlier time and place rather than using the more effective and appropriate ones occasioned by present-life situations. Since we cannot always be aware of the life events that influence and shape us, many of our memories of these events are often forgotten or repressed. Psychoanalysis is especially designed to try to recall these episodes, to retrieve our forgotten memories; and, if it can, psychoanalysis may try to reconstruct the life events and life situations which led to the psychopathological processes we suffer from today.

By helping us recall and understand how we

became who we are, by retrieving forgotten memories, by witnessing the limited ways in which we have coped with our childhood problems, psychoanalysis aims to encourage us to apply a broader range of coping mechanisms to the problems we are faced with today. Moreover, psychoanalysis helps us differentiate people, places, and situations we are dealing with today from those which we dealt with in our early formative years. In summary, understanding and insight gained during the psychoanalytic process provide us with the self-understanding and the courage to experiment with better coping methods in dealing with today's life problems.

DREAM ANALYSIS
AND INTERPRETATION

The second major component of self-analysis, after free-association, is dream analysis and interpretation. Analysis of your dreams provides valuable information about your unconscious inner conflicts.

Dream analysis, however, even with years and years of special education and training, is not easy. So be prepared for some work on understanding your own dreams. You must be patient and not expect easy or simple cookbook answers to the complexity and creativity of your own mental processes.

There are various frames of reference to be used when you work with dreams. We will have to recognize at the outset of this exploration of our psychic life by looking into the meaning of our own dreams, that there will be limits to how far we can go. Freud began to realize when he was trying to analyze his own dreams, that urges and motivations that he wanted to hide from himself because of shame, guilt, or fear, resisted discovery. And as he got stronger inklings from his dreams about some hidden psychodynamic process within himself, his motivation to work on his dreams decreased. He found that he was avoiding this work, or that he became anxious or irritable as some new understanding about himself came to light. These are the kinds of experiences associated with countertransference as well as with self-discovery.

The Dream Stimulus

We are physiologically constituted so that we dream regularly during a stage of sleep called rapid eye movement (REM) sleep, which generally occurs four times a night. The specific content of these dreams is influenced by our current life events and the psychological conflicts mobilized by them. Many psychoanalysts believe that the psychological plans, preoccupations, and conflicts of the individual are the primary factors influencing dream content. These conflicts make it inevitable that one or another aspect of the daily external events and scenes in our lives will contain something that is relevant to our current psychological preoccupations.

Many patients tell their psychoanalysts that they have had dreams that were precipitated by current events, and that they think these dreams are simply reactions to them. A skeptical psychoanalyst may question such a statement because there are many daily external events, and so how is it that only one or two of these elicited the dream? Is it not more likely that each individual may be struggling at any one time with many different psychological issues, and that the dreamer selects from the events of each day certain significant ones to which to respond? Most psychoanalysts prefer the latter explanation of the role of the dream stimulus. They believe that events in a person's life, if they can be pinpointed, arouse already latent or active psychological preoccupations. Hence, locating all the information possible about the dream stimulus will help us toward our goal in piecing out the deeper meaning of each one of our dreams.

Sigmund Freud called that portion of the preceding day's events which appears in the dreams at night the "day's residues," signifying that these events were singled out or filtered out because of their special relevance for the dreamer.

The Theory of Over-Determination of the Meaning of Dreams

A well-established theory of the hidden meanings in dreams is that the single dream carries not one idea but many different ones. This should not come as a surprise, for the memory-bank portion of our minds has a capacity greater than that of any electronic computer yet developed. We now know from scientific studies that events in our lives — what we see, hear, taste, feel, and learn — are recorded in our brains as biochemical memory traces, and that both short-term and long-term memory are probably based on chemical processes. In addition, our brains are capable of starting with the memories of every hour of our waking lives and coming up with some original and imaginative combinations of thoughts and visual pictures. These pictures, which appear in our dreams, are so real and vivid that we sometimes forget our dreams are our own constructions.

The plot of the dream, like a good poem, is highly symbolic and represents simultaneously many aspects of our own lives put together from bits and pieces of memories stored in our brain. At one level our dreams mean one thing, something very much on the surface of our present-day comprehension and our awareness. And at other levels our dreams relate to long-forgotten aspects of our childhood experience, or maybe some aspects of the collective memory of the human race. The latter idea, introduced by Carl Jung, a Swiss psychoanalyst, is a viewpoint that mankind shares a "collective unconscious"—that is, ideas and memories originating from ancestors living centuries ago. Today, scientists cannot find strong supporting evidence for all of Jung's ideas with respect to the collective unconscious. But scientists do agree that genetics and heredity are examples of an unconscious kind of memory, laid down in the biochemical composition of our genes and chromosomes in the form of complex protein molecules. These molecules, which are able to reproduce themselves, are also able to direct and give messages to the psychological and chemical processes of our body. These processes dictate that our offspring grow to human shape and form, have a human brain, have the potential of behaving in some ways and not others, and are able—unlike other life forms—to learn to speak. Today, scientists think that memories of our individual past experiences have a chemical basis in some form of protein similar to the chemical aspect of genetic memory, and that even our very earliest experiences are recorded chemically in our brain, but are not always easily recoverable.

Our present biological understanding of dreams encompasses the fact that they occur most often during a period when the brain wave patterns are similar to those of wakefulness; that our dreams are commonly associated with the filling of the blood vessels in the erectile parts of our sexual organs; and that our dreams involve a complex symbolic sensory playback, mostly in visual form, of our past life experiences. Moreover, the over-determination theory says that there is not one — and only one — interpretation of the meaning of a dream. Rather, there are many different levels of understanding the dream, some at different levels of consciousness, and others at the same level of consciousness but of differing psychological significance. This observation that there are many different messages in any one dream should ease our concern and assure us that we need not fret about finding the single true meaning of the dream.

Each dream, then, is like an unexplored island, connected perhaps — under the sea — to other incompletely explored islands and to a nearby mainland. The dream is describable from many points of view as more of the uncharted and unexplored island and its surroundings are studied. Each further exploration and each new perspective about the island adds a bit of information about the makeup of the land and its contents.

The Theory of Current and Lifetime
Psychological Conflicts in Dreams

Dream experts have discovered that dreams have some meanings that tell us about problems—external and internal—that we must currently face. These have been called "here-and-now" focal conflicts, which means circumscribed conflicts or small ones that may be very important to us now, but do not necessarily involve the main aspects of our life story or our life style. These current, immediate, here-and-now aspects of our dreams are very important to us in the immediate present and can—if understood correctly—tell us how we perceive (partly consciously and partly unconsciously) some present-life situations and emotional conflicts, and how we are trying to deal with them. These conflicts are, however, more like the individual chapters of a long book or the scenes in a long play rather than the principal theme of the whole book or play when considered altogether.

The lifetime or "nuclear" conflict portrayed in a dream, on the other hand, is one of the themes of one's life—the "story-of-my-life" part of a dream. This conflict is comparable to the main theme or message of a novel or play. The lifetime conflict depicted in a dream is a psychological one that has extended throughout much of the dreamer's existence, a conflict that evolved relatively early in his or her life. It keeps coming back in many forms as the individual faces new life experiences as well as the memories of old ones and needs to cope with them.

The nuclear conflict in the dream usually involves

the most central and deeply motivating drives in the person's life, such as the wish or need to be loved and protected, or the wish or urge to obtain recognition and to achieve a sense of usefulness and productivity. The "conflict" side of this inner struggle is manifested in anxieties rooted in childhood and in other emotional traits that provide obstacles to the realization of goals.

Naturally, our here-and-now psychological conflicts in life (and as they appear in our current dreams) are influenced by our deeper, lifetime psychological conflicts, just as a book chapter has some tie-in with the underlying theme of a novel. In fact, current conflicts are often referred to as conflicts derived from other more basic or deep lifetime psychological conflicts.

As we learn to analyze and interpret our own dreams, we should plan to look for the current (focal) conflicts in our dreams as well as the older, more basic (nuclear) conflicts in them. Also, we should prepare ourselves to find several focal and several nuclear conflicts in our dreams. It will be our intention to try to locate the most important current conflict, and to determine how the mind is trying to solve this conflict as well as how it is related to certain older ones that have left their marks on the memory system.

Common Features within the
Same Person's Dreams

A single dream, studied carefully while following the guidelines that are provided here, will give you an understanding of some aspects of the current life conflicts the dreamer is coping with and a glimpse of one of the earlier adjustment problems or conflicts in his or her life history (focal conflict). The more that is known about the dreamer's personality, lifestyle, psychodynamics, and life history, the more valid will be the interpretation of any one dream—namely, if the dreamer is you, how your dream is trying to cope with reality situations and how your dream is approaching these life problems.

Repeated studies of your dreams, naturally, can build up confidence in the accuracy and validity of the knowledge being obtained about your conscious and unconscious personality makeup, especially when a number of your different dreams provide information that supports the conclusions you have tentatively drawn from the analysis of one dream. Dream analysis can and should be done on a scientific basis. Obtaining and analyzing data from the same individual over many periods of time, and getting similar findings at different periods of observation, are ways in which scientists establish scientific truths about individual human psychology.

Of course, there are special difficulties that one encounters with scientific studies on human beings because the human organism has such a large brain for its body size, a brain capable of storing more information than that of any other life form, a brain that can put this information back together in new and creative combinations that are far beyond any electronic computer's capacity. This point is mentioned to alert the beginning dream-analyzer that the content of a series of dreams may, indeed, deal with a similar facet of a person's deeper psychology. But an occasional dream intervening in this series may deal with some other aspects of this many-faceted human being. That is, some dreams are, on the surface, different from any others in a run of dreams a person may be having. These different-faceted dreams have been evoked by the dreamer's reactions to an ongoing life experience that varies from the usual life experiences being encountered. Such an event might be an actual or possible birth, sickness or death in the family, a promotion, a potential romance, an illness, a threat to one's self-esteem, an encouraging success, a frustration in human relations, and countless other everyday life experiences. And such life events evoke from each one of us quite personalized memories and styles of psychological adaptation, which in turn may generate a unique dream experience, somewhat different from those reflecting most of our recent daily preoccupations. These facts are spelled out to warn readers not to anticipate perfect consistency in the themes of any consecutive time series of dreams; irregular and unexpected dream contents may be retrieved at any time from your less accessible memories by various life experiences that cause specific chords in these memories to resonate and become manifest.

In addition, an individual in psychoanalytic psychotherapy, or some other type of psychotherapy, who is going through a period of successful or disappointing life episodes will demonstrate prominent variations in the content of his or her dreams. This should not be unexpected, for such an individual's personality is likely to be undergoing some changes of a substantial kind (referred to by clinicians as "structural" changes); and, as a result of this, there are likely to be concomitant changes in the dream experiences.

As indicated earlier, everyone has an average of four periods of rapid eye movement sleep — or dreaming sleep—per night (except for individuals taking drugs, including alcohol, antihistamines, caffeine, and so on). Usually people do not recall as many as four dreams per night, but more likely one, two, or at the most three. The psychological conflicts, conscious and unconscious, that these dreams are dealing with are almost always identical, but the defenses and coping mechanisms in these dreams may vary. That is, the dreamer tries out several different ways of handling the emotional problems that he or she is working on during sleep. This is a helpful clue for understanding and interpreting any pair or larger number of dreams one may have during a single night; namely, to look for the arousal of a common emotional concern or theme that the dreamer is trying to work with and solve.

Dreams in large series—for example, over days or weeks—may also be dealing with the dreamer's current working preoccupations. One may, as a guide, think of chapters in a book to explore how these longer dream sequences hold together. One sentence, paragraph, or chapter never tells the whole story, in all its embellishments, of a person's deepest overall personality. But the personal uniqueness of the dreamer may begin to be revealed with one dream, and this individuality will become more definite and distinctive as more dreams are available for scrutiny.

Dream content is influenced by biological rhythms (for example, the phases of the menstrual cycle); by the use of psychoactive pharmacological agents (including drugs that are used commonly and do not require a prescription, such as alcohol, nicotine, and possibly certain vitamins); and by endocrine, metabolic, or infectious diseases. Dream content may also be affected by severe mental or emotional disorders. Nevertheless, a characteristically unique trend of personal response occurs in the dream life of each individual. For instance, a suspicious, cynical person will tend to continue to be so, regardless of the different biological factors influencing his or her mental and behavioral processes; an affectionate, hopeful person will continue to reveal these traits in his or her dreams regardless of external physiological circumstances. Exceptions to this general rule may occur in the dreams of individuals under the influence of some of the new psychoactive (mind) drugs, including tranquilizers, antidepressants, and psychotomimetic drugs (such as LSD), for these do appear to be capable of influencing the affective content or the degree of cognitive organization in dreams.

A Closer Look at Dream Work: Symbolization, Condensation, and Displacement

There are some aspects of dreams that are common to all dreams, and this gives us a basis for generalizing about the meaning of dreams and for developing a general psychology of dreams and dreaming.

Let us consider the three primary characteristics of dream work or dream psychology; namely, the processes of symbolization, condensation, and displacement.

Symbolization

There are strong evidences of similarity in the process of symbolization in poetry and literature, and also in dreams. There are no reasons for us to expect, certainly, that certain brain functions active in the waking state—such as in the creation of poetry, drama, literature, art and music — are much different from the creative processes involved in dreaming. Indeed, the innovative and original manifestations of symbolic thinking in dreaming which occur so unself-consciously and effortlessly while we dream, we would often like to be able to call upon and repeat when we are consciously trying to evoke the creative process in the waking state. Note, for example, the following symbolic features of a group of dreams:

1. A dream scene starts out on the shores of a calm sea, which builds up suddenly to a tidal wave that threatens to drown the dreamer's sisters and friends. The dreamer now becomes terrified and tries to rescue them. Analysis of the dream reveals that under the dreamer's calm exterior is a surging, powerful turmoil of emotions and urges that she is not sure she can master. The symbolism reveals that beneath a person's overt attitudes of affection there are deeper and often hostile feelings toward loved ones.

2. A dream scene depicts briefly a college student carrying a briefcase with a weapon, a gun, hidden inside it. Dream analysis reveals that the dreamer feels aggressively competitive with his fellow students. The dream symbolism tells that under this person's guise of intellectual and academic pursuit is a hidden rivalry with his fellow students that is as dangerous as a gun can be.

3. A dream scene has a 16-year-old girl, the dreamer, partially blinded "because God has taken away His protection" from her. Dream analysis reveals that she and her father had shared a vacation together, during which the father and daughter had many long,

pleasant conversations. He gave her some advice concerning her everyday worries that she found very helpful. When the vacation came to an end, the girl missed her father's companionship and the insights he had provided. The dream symbolism makes the father all-knowing and all-powerful, like God the Father; and it equates becoming blind with no longer obtaining insights and understanding (to not see = to not know).

4. In the next dream, a small baby boy was climbing huge steps and looking for his mother. He finally found her upstairs in a dark place, standing very close to his father and unresponsive to his cries. In reporting the dream, the dreamer felt an uncontrollable urge to cry and developed some transient, itching wheals, usually called "hives," on his skin. Dream analysis revealed that the dreamer was experiencing a deep sense of withdrawal of approval and of unfair criticism by a review board, and that his feeling of righteous indignation was incapable of actually correcting the error. The symbolism eloquently likens the dreamer's psychological situation to that of a baby boy scaling mountainous steps to reach a supporting mother; even when he finally locates her she is preoccupied with someone else and deaf to his entreaties. (The urge to cry and the skin hives have no symbolic significance, but are occasional psychophysiological accompaniments to feelings of desertion and hopeless rage.)

Condensation

Condensation is another facet of the mental transformations occurring in dreaming. It is similar and related to the process of symbolization, for both of these processes may involve the use of a certain amount of mental shorthand to represent more complex and detailed memories, perceptions, cognitions, and emotions. Condensation refers, specifically, to the representation of the whole of a psychological experience by a part. Our spoken language permits this process to some extent by supplying us with demonstrative pronouns (such as "this, that, these, those") and indefinite pronouns (such as "it"); these words may refer to complex series of life events (for example, in the statement "it was intolerable," where "it" refers to ten years of living in Detroit or two years of dating a boyfriend). Our spoken language also makes readily possible our representing many phenomena or ideas by single words, such as words referring to genera rather than species (for example, *fish* rather than trout, or *mammal* rather than elephant); collective nouns (such as *crowds, millennia, century, infinity*); and nouns or pronouns referring to constructs rather than concrete objects (*wartime* rather than soldier, *beauty* rather than you, and so forth). In addition, there is a figure of speech ("synecdoche") which permits a whole idea to be represented by a part: the use of the word "sail" to represent a whole ship.

An added feature of dreaming is that most dreams are composed of visual rather than auditory imagery. This means that visual sequences, to a greater extent than sequences based on other sensory modalities, represent the thought and the emotional content that the dream is portraying. Hence, shading and color may signify various characteristics. Moreover, brief or even trivial dream sequences may summarize a major aspect of the dreamer's lifestyle, some typical relationship with other people, or a habitual psychological conflict. Such sequences illustrate the process of condensation in dreaming. A few illustrations follow:

1. In a long series of the dreams of one individual, some person in each dream was made fun of or ridiculed. This theme was a condensation of the dreamer's lifelong attitude toward her father or any man who reminded her of him.

2. A dream about dribbling a basketball and throwing it through a hoop proved to represent a condensation of conflictual masturbation fantasies.

3. A woman's dream of receiving a blood transfusion which was inadequate to help her weakened state was found to represent her unconscious wish that her husband would give her the love and support she felt deprived of since childhood, and her feeling of despair that this "shot in the arm" or "refueling" would ever be sufficient.

4. A dream depicted a young man trying to locate and possibly rescue a young woman swimming under the water. Dream analysis indicated that this represented his search for his mother, who had died when he was a child, and his tendency to look for impossible degrees of satisfaction whenever frustrated in his sexual life or even his vocation.

Displacement

The third dream process described here is the psychological defense or coping mechanism of displacement; namely, the process by which one directs an unacceptable need or urge to a different object or objects than the original one(s). This psychological process enables forbidden urges or wishes to be disguised in dreams by having them occur to unidentified persons, or to recognizable people other than the self. The mechanism of displacement makes it possible for any dream character to represent some portion or portions of the dreamer. Understanding the dream stimulus, the free associations, and other details about the dreamer can help to clarify which other people or psychological parts of the dreamer are represented by the dreams.

Some examples of displacement in dreams have already been given in previous dream samples described herein. Let us examine a few additional illustrations.

1. A young wife was deeply troubled by an impending temporary separation from her husband, who was scheduled to be gone for two weeks on a business trip. Reared by her parents, particularly her father, to believe that self-sufficiency was a virtue and dependency a weakness, and taught as a small child that being comforted and hugged when she was crying was unlikely to happen, she acted indifferent under these circumstances; however, she felt vaguely uncomfortable and had difficulty sleeping soundly at night.

She dreamed that an acquaintance of her husband's had died and that she was trying to locate a good physician for him. Then the dead person phoned her and told her that the doctor she wanted to get for him was sick and dying and that he was not very competent as a physician anyway. In this dream the dreamer had displaced her unacceptable (to her) distress at being separated from her husband to her husband's acquaintance, thereby equating separating with dying. She also displaced her repressed anger at her husband (and originally her father) to the doctor, making him "sick and dying" and "not very competent." The dead person calling her on the phone represented a wish not to be alienated from her husband (or father), and, hence, a magical return of her husband (as if from the dead). Her continued negative feelings toward persons who would not allow her the open expression of her emotions, and who deprived her of her dependency needs, are revealed in that portion of the dream content that indicated that the doctor was not a very competent one. Usually, displacements of these kinds in dreams indicate negative and/or positive feelings that the dreamer is also having toward his or her self.

2. A young man reported a short dream. He parked his auto, and on his return he found that someone had stolen one of his front tires. The auto turned out to be a displacement of (or substitution for) himself. The loss of a "front tire" symbolically represented his feeling that there was an impairment of his ability to take decisive responsibility for a course of action that he preferred. To know whether he had deprived himself of the ability to steer his actions where he desired, or whether someone else was the culprit, would require considerably more information than we have available here.

3. A 5-year-old boy had a nightmare of being pursued by an angry lion. The lion was a displacement of the child's own angry feelings. He had been disciplined by his mother in order to make him control his temper and refrain from saying bad things to her. A child at this age is developing a conscience (ego-ideal and super-ego) and is usually working toward mastering

hostile impulses. He fears the open expression of his anger that may lead to the mother's disapproval and loss of love. Hence, in the dream this child disowns his own anger and then becomes fearful of his own angry impulses which are displaced to a wild beast. Could the angry lion possibly also represent an angry mother or father at the same time? Yes, especially if there is evidence that either one of these parents has bared fangs, unsheathed claws, and growled a number of times at the child.

4. A woman had a dream in which she took a walk along a dark street, and a man whom she recognized approached and made sexual advances toward her. When she refused him, he tried to rape her, and she awakened in a state of fright.

The analysis of this dream revealed that the dreamer had unconscious wishes to have sexual relations with this man, but felt ashamed and guilty about these impulses. She had displaced her own sexual impulses to the man, putting herself in the passive rather than active position. As a potential rape victim, with the sexual aggression forced onto her, she could help ease her conscience. If she were forced to have sexual relations and thereby possibly got hurt, how could it be said that she had enjoyed these intimate relations? The dreamer was awakened by her anxiety in this dream because she was partially aware of her own conflicting erotic impulses, and also because she did not want badly enough to be hurt in the process.

5. A displacement similar to the previous one occurred repetitively in the case of a pretty young woman who had anxiety dreams that an unknown man was

hiding under her bed. Her husband, a successful traveling salesman, was away from home during the week. She had displaced her sexual longings for her absent husband, to a hidden and unknown man. The externalization of her inner needs to someone else relieved her shame about her own sexual needs; however, now she had to cope with her own hidden sexual passions displaced to an unfamiliar man, which violated her feelings of loyalty to her husband.

In summary, dreams are psychological and physiological events in our lives that occur primarily during the second stage of four levels of sleep. Our dreams are accompanied by stimulation of our involuntary nervous systems, especially if the dreams contain much emotional content. Very little muscular activity occurs during dreaming, except the following of the dream's action with our eyes. The content of dreams can reveal considerable information about our deeper worries and conflicts.

This next section deals with how one can go about making headway on analyzing one's own dreams.

Recalling and Writing Down Dreams

It is possible to improve one's dream recall by firmly resolving to study one's dreams and recall them. For some people, writing paper and a pencil by the bedside will increase the incentive to write down the contents of dreams during the night, especially if one is awakened by the dream; or to write down the dream in the morning, before the events and activities of the day interfere with dream recall. It is important to put down every detail, no matter how apparently trivial.

If a sleeper has had two or three or more dreams during the night, these should be written down in the order in which they were dreamt. The setting or context of the dream, the background in the dream, the number of characters and what they look like and what they did or said or implied, and whether the dream was in color or in black and white—all these details and many others should be noted.

Listing Subjective Feelings during Different Phases of the Dreams

There should now be added, to the detailed report of each dream, a self-analysis of the subjective feelings that the dreamer experienced to each situation or activity in the dream. That is, the dreamer should ask him- or herself, after awakening, whether there was any awareness that any character in the dream had subjective feelings that reminded the dreamer of his or her own. The dreamer should write down any subjective feelings experienced during different phases of the dream by any character in the dream other than the person who most clearly represents the dreamer. These subjective feelings and their recall provide clues toward understanding the significance of the dream in greater depth. Their recall often helps recover other portions of the dream content that have slipped away from awareness.

Determining the Dream Stimulus

In locating the dream stimulus, to start with, it is enough to ask ourselves what happened during the day preceding the dreaming or what has been happening over the past week or several days that seems important or crucial. Searching for these details may prove more fruitful if one casually goes over what seem to have been the important occurrences in one's life. If there are several such events, the next step is to see whether these have some common denominator or whether they are highly unrelated kinds of events. The next step is to note the feelings one had about these events, both the active urge or motivation and the counteraction to it; for example, a wish to climb a mountain for excitement and adventure, which may be in conflict with a fear of personal injury.

It is a good idea to jot down those ideas about current events which appear to have some connection with the possible dream stimulus. We will be using this information later on to pinpoint more accurately what psychological significance our dream does indeed have.

Free Association on the Dream

To accomplish the next step in our dream analysis, we have to do some private free-associating. Sigmund Freud taught his patients to free-associate by instructing them with the "fundamental rule." These instructions request that the person try as hard as possible to overlook the usual censorship that is exercised over his or her marginal thoughts, feelings, and wishes, to speak up freely about whatever comes to mind, and to continue this process by uncritically letting come to his or her mind every memory provoked by the preceding thoughts. To get the best results in free-associating one has to suspend one's usual moral or

ethical judgments, perspectives, and preferences, and
allow to come to awareness any thoughts, feelings, or
wishes at all that might be directly or indirectly related
to what one is momentarily concentrating on. While
one is so doing, one should not keep out of awareness
any bodily sensations or experiences. Rather these
should also be brought to awareness and studied in
more detail, for even bodily sensations have some
connection with feelings and thoughts we may have
hidden from ourselves.

Free-Associating on the Whole Dream

One should consider the whole dream and allow to
flood into one's mind every thought, feeling, desire,
and memory that may then happen to come along.
These may be jotted down for later reference.

Free-Associating on Dream Elements

After free-associating and noting all one can in this
connection with the whole dream, then one should take
even the most minute details of the dream and make a
note of (actually or mentally) every experience or idea
or urge that one is reminded of by considering each one
of these tiny details. Many dreams contain, in themselves, psychological issues or conflicts, and if these are
obvious the dream-analyst has a very helpful lead into
the significance of the dream. He or she should thus
free-associate as actively and productively as possible to
bring up whatever memories, ideas, and feelings can be
retrieved.

Free-Associating on Any Unusual Events or Details in Dreams

Quite often our dreams have funny or ridiculous details or unexplained features that help us distinguish the kind of thinking that occurs with dreaming and sleeping from that which occurs during wakefulness. These usually provide an important clue as to the deeper, more hidden meaning of our dreams.

Searching for Common Themes

With the dream stimulus, the dream manifest content, and the data of your free associations (dream latent content) loosely in your mind, now let your mind play lightly over these separate dream facets. Without too much pressure on your thinking process, search for themes, common denominators associated with the dream stimulus, manifest dream content, and latent dream content. If you locate one apparently common theme, quickly make a note of it. And then, similarly, look for a possible second theme. Note this. Next look for the more common themes that seem to connect one dream facet to another. Note these. You can be confident that these common themes, themes that overlap through all features of the dream, are substantial leads and clues to the current psychological conflicts with which your dream is dealing.

Formulating the Psychological Conflicts Revealed in the Dream

Having noted these common themes running through the dream stimulus, the dream manifest content, and your free associations to your dream, we are ready to try to outline the current psychological conflicts that have led to the dream script and subject matter. Remember that psychological conflicts include some kind of wish, desire, urge, or need, and an opposing motive (an emotion, attitude, or value orientation) that was aroused by the initial urge or drive.

We may now have enough information to arrive at some ideas of both the current psychological conflict and deeper, older lifetime conflicts revealed in the dream.

Examples of Dream Analysis and Interpretation

Let us look at some examples of dream analysis to get our bearings on how to proceed.

Example 1

Dream Stimulus   "My friend J. at work got a salary raise the day preceding the dream, and I did not. I congratulated my friend and covered up my envy."

Manifest Dream   "Some familiar-looking person had an accident on the highway and almost hit my car in the process. I was able to avoid being struck. I did not have time to wait to find out the identity or fate of the driver. So I kept on driving to work."

Free Associations   "The dream sequence is strange, for it is not like me to shirk a responsibility to help a fellow driver out of possible injury. The other auto in the dream had struck a stop sign on the roadside and abruptly came to a halt. The front of the car was smashed in."

"I could not figure out the make of the other car. It was a bright red, though. My friend J. had gotten a new car, two-toned red and yellow. He was boasting about getting a bigger paycheck than I. He has been a good friend of mine, but somehow I have not liked associating with him much anymore. I cannot clearly recall any feeling I had in the dream except that I was a little irritated that this other car nearly ran into mine. The other feeling was an urgent one that I had to get to my job as soon as I could because something very important was going on there. Maybe it was something like guilt. I don't know. It is not clear at all what it was."

Dream Analysis and Interpretation

Common Themes In waking life, the dreamer's friend J. made progress on the job and the dreamer did not. In the dream, the dreamer made uninterrupted progress in his auto while an unknown driver came to an abrupt halt and was probably hurt.

We will, from now on, assume that the various themes we can perceive running through the dream stimulus, the manifest dream, and the dreamer's association, constitute the dreamer's conscious or unconscious motives, urges, or wishes. These various motives can be listed as:

Motive 1: Wish to get recognition and a salary raise, which were both given to a friend and not to dreamer (a wish frustrated by reality).

Motive 2: Envy of a friend's success, an emotion not quite acceptable to the dreamer.

Motive 3: Urge to injure a friend (out of envy at his success), an impulse which is completely unacceptable.

Motive 4: Fear of retaliation from a friend (for having hostile urge toward him).

Motive 5: Unconscious guilt feelings originating from the dreamer's hostile feelings toward a friend (because having such a hostile urge does not fit dreamer's moral code).

In the dream, the dreamer covers up the identity of his friend (dream solution to conflicting motives) and makes him a stranger (due to guilt over urge to be hostile to friend). The dreamer pictures his friend having an auto accident and having his forward motion stopped instead of these events occurring to the dreamer (an expression of the dreamer's hostile wish to "get ahead" of his friend); but in the process the dreamer (his car) almost got hit (fear of retaliation for hostile urge toward friend).

The dreamer unconsciously wishes to damage the front end of his friend (that is, his virility — this is sometimes referred to as a "castration wish"), but the dreamer fears retaliation from his own conscience for this hostile wish. The dreamer does not wish to get hurt, but there is fear of retaliation for his wishing harm to his friend. Also, his guilt over his envy of and anger at his friend makes the whole thought sequence unacceptable to the dreamer. So the dream process changes an intolerable emotional struggle to an impersonal (isolation) accident scene (symbolization) on the highway involving some auto driver the dreamer does not know (displacement).

Current Psychological Conflict   The current conflict of the above dream example would be the wish to have a salary increase, a wish that is frustrated by the reality of the dreamer's friend, which in turn mobilizes both the fear of retaliation and a feeling of guilt.

Lifetime Psychological Conflict   The lifetime conflict would include the destructive aggressive urge (id impulse) to destroy a successful friend, an urge that conflicts with guilt and with fear of retaliation (superego reaction). It is likely that this conflict is the older and more general one. The focal conflict (the wish to get more salary conflicts with no salary increase for self but one for a friend) is a variant of the nuclear conflict in this example, but need not always be so.

Example 2

Dream Stimulus   "My psychiatrist, a man in whom I have confided a great deal, announced yesterday he was going on a two-week vacation and he will not be available to see me."

Manifest Dream   "I had a very simple dream. I was looking at a newspaper headline in very big print. It said 'Detective Shot and Killed!' That's all there was to the dream . . . I had no feeling at all about the headline except that here was another matter of violence in the big city."

Free Associations   "There are a distressing number of shootings of police officers in this city. Actually, the newspaper headline was about a detective, a law officer who investigates criminal behavior. I think of Sherlock

Holmes, the master detective who was able to solve many mysterious and puzzling cases that baffled others.

"My psychiatrist, in a way, is a detective, looking for clues to the secrets of my mind.

"But why would I dream he was shot and killed? I don't dislike him. Could I feel angry with him? I know he's going on a vacation and will be away. It is unbelievable that I would want him killed for this. The thought comes to my mind that the best defense is a strong offense. Would I want someone to get him first so that I wouldn't feel victimized by being cut off by him?

"In truth, I don't really mind missing some treatment sessions with him. What pops into my mind is that this situation with him is vaguely similar to an earlier one in my life when I was 8 and my father accused me of taking my younger brother's marbles. It wasn't true, and I was hurt and angry with my father over this episode. I didn't dare talk back to him, though, for he didn't tolerate anything of this sort.

"I recall I was a little jealous of my younger brother's good looks and my mother's obvious affection for him. But he and I got along well."

Dream Analysis and Interpretation

Common Themes   The departure or separation from the dreamer of a significant male in his life, by fair or foul means.

> *Motive 1*:   The dreamer has a wish to be dependent on the psychiatrist, about which he feels ashamed.

Motive 2:   Furthermore, he feels murderous anger at his psychiatrist for planning to go away on vacation, and this anger arouses the dreamer's guilt feelings.

Motive 3:   The dreamer's shame over his dependency on a parental figure and his guilt over his murderous rage lead to trying to forget (suppression and repression) of these unacceptable urges.

Current Psychological Conflict   The urge to destroy a frustrating father figure (the psychiatrist cannot be completely put out of the dreamer's awareness), an impulse that returns in a disguised form as a murderous act toward a complete stranger (displacement), an unknown detective (symbolization).

Lifetime Psychological Conflict   The dreamer had normal early childhood dependency urges toward his mother and father. He also had some envy of his younger brother and his possessions, which the dreamer was taught not to express. His wish to be the preferred child in the family was frustrated by his father's unwarranted accusations that he took possessions (marbles) from his younger brother. This life situation led to the arousal of murderous wishes toward his father for his inaccurate "detective" work about the stealing of marbles, and for the father's implicit repudiation of him. He suffered guilt over his murderous urges toward his father. The current and lifetime conflicts aroused by the dreamer's psychiatrist interrupting treatment to take a vacation are neatly encapsulated in an emotionally neutralized newspaper headline concerning a detective being shot and killed (condensation).

Following a Series of Your Dreams

As have already been pointed out, a single dream carefully studied will give an understanding of some of the current psychological conflicts with which one is coping, but only a hint of the older lifetime conflicts that one has had to face. The analysis of many dreams from the same individual, on the other hand, can give a fuller view of these lifetime conflicts, while illustrating the variety of psychological maneuvers the dreamer uses to adjust to stressful day-to-day situations.

Example 1

The analysis of a series of another individual's dreams is useful to help one achieve a more thorough view of oneself, including the complexities of one's personality and the extent to which one's adjustment patterns can change with time or in response to a therapeutic agent. As a beginning, let us study a short series of dreams from one young man, a college student. Unfortunately, we have no free associations on these dreams so we have no way to look into the extent to which, and in what ways, these dreams have undergone some distortion and covering up (secondary elaboration) of the original manifest dream content. Without free associations we will be somewhat hindered from getting at the latent dream content. The dreams all occurred within a one-week period and were written down by the dreamer, a student in his early twenties who lived at home with his parents. He had very little social life and was shy with women. He aspired to be a writer or movie director.

Dream Series 1

Dream Stimulus   The dreamer had just sought his father's opinion about his desire to quit college and get a job, though he had never before had any gainful employment.

Dream 1   "A girl was telling me to be more frank with my father and to tell him of my reservations about the helpfulness of his advice regarding my dropping out of school."

Dream 2   "I was in the mountains, this was around the time of my high school days, and I was being hunted down by Indians. They had bows and arrows, and one almost got me. I was afraid the Indians would cut my throat. The scene changed and I was at my high school, and I was running in between houses, trying to get away from the Indians. My friend Charlie was with me, and I asked how he planned to get away. He said he was trying to go it on his own and escape solo. I said, 'I have tried that but you know, you get hungry after a while.' Charlie laughed.

"Next scene was at an eating area where we could get a free dinner. Charlie was sitting about four seats away on a bench. The guy ahead of him wiped some food on Charlie's face and said, 'Pass it on.' This piece of food eventually found its way to the chap next to me, and after taking a sample of it, he put it on my face and spoke the words, 'Pass it on.' I decided not to pass it on, but placed it back on the guy who had put it on me, and said, 'What's this about?' "

Dream 3   "Again, this dream went back to the time I was with Charlie. We went into a store with the plan of getting some grass. The woman there laid it on the counter, I gave her $20, she took it and confusedly returned about $40 to me. Then an oldish couple walked into the store, and they looked like narks. So Charlie and I just left the stuff on the counter and walked out."

Dream 4   "Inside some auditorium, there was a girl with her boyfriend and he was in his late twenties and had a full beard. We were going to play some records, and I had some of my albums there, and I went through them to see which to play that might impress them. Then another girl was there laughing and making a pass at me. I had somewhere picked up somebody's key chain, and on it was a nude female figure. The girl looked at it and laughed. Then later on I had to leave the auditorium. When I came back, I was afraid some of my record albums were stolen. I checked, and some were."

Dream 5   "This dream started on a street, it was at night, and police were walking down the street with guns and started arresting many people. I ran and turned the corner and the panicked, crowded throbbing night scene changed.

"There was an old store, and a young girl with big eyes looked at me and asked if she could stay with me. Then her mother came up to me, and I said, 'You have an aggressive daughter.' I acted kind of cool and wanted to show the mom that I was no tough guy. But at the same time, I wanted to take the little girl home.

The mother left, and then I looked at the girl and motioned for her to follow me. She started to follow me and then hesitated. At this point, I woke up.

"At the beginning of this dream, some of these people and I seemed to be up on a mock stage. I can't recall what we were doing up there, but I remember that there were a lot of people around watching us, and we were having a great time."

Since we do not have access to the dreamer's free associations about these dreams, although we do have an event just preceding the dreams that probably served as a stimulus for them, we will look for common themes only in the dream stimulus and all the ensuing dreams. This will give us some general ideas concerning what inner needs and conflicts this dreaming activity was trying to deal with.

Common Themes

With the dream stimulus, the young man is faced with the problem of justifying to his father his desire to discontinue his education and get a job. In so doing, he recognizes the fact that he has had no previous experience in gainful employment.

Dream 1   The dreamer has someone—a girl—advising him that he should be more open about his dislike of his father's efforts to help him come to a decision about dropping out of school. There is a suggestion that he is covering up his true feelings about his father's advice. Unfortunately, we do not know, from the information we have to work with, what the father's advice really was.

Dream 2   There is a fear of being killed by arrows or throat-cutting (oral reference) at the hands of wild Indians (an expression of his severe conscience, his superego, which is displaced to others). Just what the urge or motivation is that is evoking such a strong reaction from his conscience in the form of a fear of retaliation is not clear at this point. Apparently, the unacceptable motivation is embedded in his wish to drop out of college. Possibly, the fear of getting his throat cut provides a clue, in that he sensed (unconsciously) some urge associated with the throat and feeding, getting fed, or being nurtured (symbolization), and dropping out of school.

In his isolation and loneliness, he changes the scene to one in which he has a companion, Charlie (misery loves company), with whom he is sharing the punishment of conscience.

Some joking and humor are provided in this dream, easing the emotional strain he is apparently experiencing, and this humor is supposed to help him deal with what we discover is "hunger" (burdened with possible shame). It appears that there is something about this hunger that makes him worry about suffering the attacks of his unbridled conscience (wild Indians) in the company of a male companion, rather than alone.

The theme of becoming hungry and getting free food is now clearly introduced (possibly representing the dreamer's continuing wish to be on the receiving end and be supplied with support from his father or any other available sources).

A slapstick quality now develops in the dreaming process with the idea of men eating together by smearing food on each other's faces (more use of wit and humor to deal with difficult inner problems). In addition, the dreamer comes up with the argument that he is not alone or unique in wanting to be fed, for many other men, as well as he, line up for free food (which serves to decrease his own shame about wanting to be taken care of). A hint that this feeding chain—and everything it may symbolize—is not entirely comfortable to him is again provided by his not going along with all of it.

Dream 3   The theme of getting something for nothing recurs—he is about to get some marijuana and money free. In Dream 1 a girl and a father gave him something: advice. In Dream 2, free food was made available.

The theme of companionship recurs—he is not alone, but with Charlie.

The theme of getting caught in an illegal action (getting an illegal substance which is taken by mouth for pleasure) is introduced. This may, however, reflect the idea that his wish to quit school has an illegal component (at least for his conscience), which was already hinted at in Dream 2 when he dreamt about Indians wanting to cut his throat.

The theme of covering up recurs, and now it is reflected in the hidden oral aims that he and his friend want to disown in the presence of some older (parental) couple, the "narks."

Dream 4   Now there appears a wish to impress a young couple by playing his records (mild exhibitionistic urge for attention).

The theme of getting something free reappears—

this time in the form of a girl who may be offering him sex. Borrowing or taking somebody's key chain with a nude woman on it is a puzzling detail, suggesting perhaps that he needs some other male along with him to back him up on a heterosexual enterprise.

The theme of someone stealing his records is similar to previous references to the possible hostility toward him of other people, such as the wild Indians, the "narks," and (in Dream 5) the police. (That this may represent fear of retaliation for his own acquisitiveness, and, hence, projection of his own urges, is a possibility. But it also may indicate a primary distrust in the reliability and predictability of others.)

Dream 5   Policemen with guns and the need to run away in this dream constitute a familiar theme.

The wish to have a girl seek him out sexually (a wish to be provided for with minimal effort on his part) is familiar. The covering up of his real intentions or feelings (in this dream, from the girl's mother) has occurred in previous dreams. The wish to dramatize himself and be exhibitionistic (as if on stage) is familiar. It jibes with his serious interest in becoming a movie director.

> *Motive 1*:   Wish to discontinue his college education and get a job.
>
> *Motive 2*:   Fear of severe punishment for his unacceptable urges.
>
> *Motive 3*:   Wish for free food, free sex, and free marijuana — that is, without any obligation.
>
> *Motive 4*:   Wish for companionship with others,

especially men, to share his pleasures and punishments.

Motive 5:   Fear of people stealing his possessions.

Motive 6:   Need to cover up his motives or feelings, especially from father and mother figures.

Motive 7:   Wish to show off or dramatize self or be
recognized publicly

Current Psychological Conflicts

The dreamer wants to discontinue his college
education and get a job but he fears his father will
disapprove. His grades are poor and he is smoking a lot
of marijuana. His own conscience gives him a much
tougher time on this issue than does his father, for in
his dreams he fancies himself being hunted down and
in danger of being killed by Indians or policemen.
(This is a manifestation of his superego.)

Underlying his wish to quit college and take a job
is a more childlike motivation to be taken care of like a
little boy who gets many goodies free or with very little
effort on his part. He is ashamed of these aspects of his
plan to quit school, and he prefers to keep these hidden.
Also, he has a guilty conscience about these urges to be
dependent and to have all his wants be taken care of.
He fears and expects physical punishment just for
thinking and dreaming about these desires.

Somehow, despite the dilemma of these conflicting
aims, the dreamer is able to draw on some unknown
personality resources and add a touch of humor, even
slapstick comedy, to these situations. It is apparent that
this shy, reserved, and lonely young man, who aspires

to be a playwright or a movie director, lessens the severity of his conflicts by giving himself some companionship in his dreams and playing with the idea that maybe the dreams are only play-acting instead of the real thing.

Lifetime Psychological Conflicts

Without some data about the dreamer's life history and some of his own free associations we will not be able to document how long-standing are some of the conflicts and coping mechanisms that have been discussed under Current Psychological Conflicts. We can be sure, however, that there must be a past history to some of the recurring behaviors pictured in the dreams. It is a safe guess that high standards for achievement were set for him by his parents, (and that, hence, he has a strict conscience with respect to achieving goals once set); that he was well indulged and taken care of as a child (and thus longs to recapture this childhood paradise of plenty without effort); and that he has been a person who typically covers up his true feelings.

Shame and guilt feelings at not achieving academic or other goals must be long-standing psychological conflicts for this dreamer.

Recurrent Dreams

Some people have recurrent dreams; that is, dreams that have exactly the same or similar themes and that are dreamt repeatedly. These repetitive dreams are common in childhood, but adults not infrequently report having dreams of this sort, too.

Do these repetitive dreams have biological and psychological bases different from those of the dreams that have been described thus far? Do these kinds of dreams signify something different from dreams in which the manifest content or theme is not very similar to that of other dreams?

Repetitive dreams are like nonrepetitive dreams with respect to their biological and psychodynamic bases. But repetitive dreams are different in that the psychological conflicts at the root of the theme are not changed by having the dream itself or by intervening waking events — such as, for example, psychotherapy or good fortune — that might otherwise help resolve the oppressive psychological dilemmas contributing to the dream story or dream content. That is, the dreamer is continuing to be faced with the same urges and goals and anxieties associated with these dilemmas and has developed no new ways of dealing with them. There may be several reasons why the dreamer has not increased his skills or abilities to enable himself to modify or improve his ways of dealing with these psychological conflicts:

1. The dreamer is simply not aware of the nature of the inner psychological conflicts producing the dream story, and, hence, is unable to work on trying out different solutions to these personal problems.

2. The dreamer has some inkling of the psychological conflicts which are bothering him, but does not know what to do about the conflicts or how to change his approach to them. Young children are often in this situation because they have relatively little control over the rules and regulations which affect their daily lives,

but rather are subject to their parents' control. More-over, their range of coping mechanisms in regard to the ordinary problems of living are limited; for example, problems in the areas of impulse versus control, inde-pendence versus dependence, trust versus distrust, and so forth. Adults are also sometimes in situations which they cannot change or avoid, and which trigger or expose them to problems they cannot readily solve; for example, sexual temptations, fear of desertion or with-drawal of support, or inescapable pressures against the expression of anger or rage.

3. The emotions aroused by some life event or events are so overwhelming or catastrophic that the memories associated with the experience are indelibly etched in one's mind. Such memories may return to haunt the dreamer with even slight provocation. During wakefulness the dreamer is easily reminded by everyday events of this catastrophe, which may include the death of a loved one or a threat to one's own continued existence. Since the range of effective psy-chological coping mechanisms for such situations is limited, and lies more in the direction of passive resignation and mourning rather than active mastering and overcoming, one's dreams about such events are not likely to have much variation in theme.

Nonrepetitive dreams, on the other hand, usually do not have these background characteristics. The following examples of repetitive dreams illustrate these features:

Example 1

A woman had a 4-year-old son who developed a fatal kidney disease. For a brief time he seemed to be responding to hospital treatment, but one day when the mother went to the hospital to visit her little boy, she found him lying in bed dead. She picked up his body and held it close to her to try to revive him, though the physician-in-charge had already declared him dead and signed the death certificate. She refused to surrender the boy's body and cried loudly and endlessly. Finally, she was persuaded by her husband to give up her son's body and leave the hospital.

As a result of this experience, she had a nervous breakdown, characterized by inconsolable grief, that required a period of treatment in a mental hospital. On discharge from the hospital and periodically for more than ten years thereafter, she had vivid nightmares with the following theme:

Recurrent Dream 1   She clearly saw her son lying dead in bed exactly as she had found him the day she went to the hospital. There was no other action or scene in this vivid dream. She was definitely the person looking at the dead boy. She felt overwhelmed by a painful sense of loss and intense grief as she gazed at the child. The dream invariably awakened her in a fit of crying. This example particularly illustrates No. 3 in the preceding list of reasons for recurrent dreams—namely, the potential of a catastrophic event, that one has no easy method of handling psychologically, to trigger such dreams. Recurring threats to one's own life, prisoner-of-war or refugee camp experiences, and so forth, can also precipitate the occurrence of repetitive dreams in certain individuals.

The mother who lost her toddler son tried to handle her recurring nightmare by staying up all night and taking light naps during the day. When this did not absolutely prevent her from dreaming, she began taking whatever varieties of psychomotor stimulant drugs she could get from several different physicians, or over-the-counter drugs at her neighborhood pharmacy, so that she could stay awake several days at a time; then she would take several sleeping pills to try to sleep so deeply she would not dream. This approach did not work to her advantage either, for she still occasionally had her nightmare. In this connection, there is evidence that nightmares often occur during the fourth stage of sleep, rather than during rapid eye movement (REM) stage-two sleep. This poor woman finally got relief from her repetitive nightmare through psychotherapy that was designed to help her more effectively complete her mourning and give up her attachment to the son who had died so many years ago.

Recently, scientists have learned that certain types of minor tranquilizers called "benzodiazepines" specifically suppress stage-four sleep, and may thus be helpful in relieving the victims of nightmares, whether or not the nightmares are repetitive in theme. The use of such pharmacologic agents by themselves may assist in suppressing the occurrence of a nightmare, but will have no favorable influence on the dreamer's psychological need to have such dreams in the first place. At this time in our knowledge, only psychotherapy suffices to remedy the underlying pathological depression associated with a grief reaction.

Example 2

A college student reported the following dream which had occurred repeatedly over many years:

Recurrent Dream 2   "I am being flown in an airplane and the person flying the plane is unknown to me, and the whole experience is very frightening to me."

The only comment that the student had to offer that might serve as a clue related to the historical background of this recurrent dream was that her parents had been divorced when she was 10 years old. Several years before and after this period, she had lived for brief occasions with her maternal grandmother or a paternal aunt and uncle instead of with either parent.

The manifest dream content puts the patient in a situation high off the ground, a situation that is not itself considered perilous during this age of air travel. It does symbolize, however, considerable distance from the relative safety of having one's "feet on the ground" and being close to so-called "Mother Earth." The act of flying, on the other hand, could be exciting or exhilarating, as it often is perceived to be in dreams symbolizing sexual desire and stimulation or the enjoyable feelings associated with a newly developed ability to be independent or with the mastery of some difficult problem. But our dreamer experiences this dream as a frightening one with the implications that one could fall from a great height and be hurt. This is a common emotional reaction embedded in the kind of anxiety psychiatrists refer to as "separation anxiety," an overly strong fear involving a real or imagined threat of the loss of support or love from someone upon whom one customarily relies.

The uncertainty about who is piloting the plane makes the dream situation even more precarious, and corroborates the idea that the dreamer keeps being preoccupied with two questions: Whose hands is she in now, and what is the identity and the nature of the commitment of the person entrusted with the guardianship of her life and fate?

Current Psychological Conflict

An event has recently occurred that makes this person think of being independent and self-sufficient, but because she feels she lacks the know-how to manage this confidently herself, she passively puts herself in the care or under the guidance of someone else. The identity and reliability of the person she depends on always seems to be in question and this makes her fearful of being misled or dropped.

Long-Term Psychological Conflict

The childhood distress she suffered with respect to who was going to be responsible for parenting her, with her real parents quarreling and separating, has left her with an indelible worry. Children at the age of 10 or younger often wish they could be on their own and manage without relying on parental rule or whim, but they invariably discover that the complexities of life, especially in our society, make them ill-equipped to succeed on their own. Hence, they are obliged to be dependent on whoever will take responsibility for them.

This recurrent dream tells us that the dreamer experienced insecurity and repeated separation anxiety as a child, regarding who would be her parent or parental substitute. As a young adult, she is unconsciously reminded of this childhood dilemma. She has

this recurrent dream whenever new steps toward independent thinking or action have to be taken or whenever someone seems to threaten her normal needs for
support or love.

Limitations in the Analysis of One's Own Dreams

Some of the pitfalls in the analysis of one's own dreams
that Freud learned about are applicable to the self-
analysis of dreams today. These obstacles rarely
present themselves in obvious ways during the analysis
of a few dreams. Rather, they begin to show up when
one begins to fathom the depths of one's mind by
continuing exploration and analysis of one's dreams.
Some of these pitfalls are the following:

1. There are likely to be certain disturbing urges or
impulses expressed in one's dreams that the dreamer
does not want to know about.

I believe that anyone selecting a book of this sort to
read and study is motivated toward self-knowledge and
self-understanding. But as one proceeds toward these
goals, there are internal obstacles that hinder one's
reaching them. These hindrances are acquired, having
been learned sometime during our lives, and they tell
us that we are bad, wicked, shameful, or otherwise
unlovable for having certain kinds of motivations or
desires. For many of us merely the thought or feeling of
any one of these unacceptable wishes is the same as the
deed — that is, the same as carrying out any action
associated with the thought or urge. The Ten Com-
mandments and the Seven Deadly Sins (Pride, Covet-
ousness, Lust, Envy, Gluttony, Anger, and Sloth or

Indolence) include some of these forbidden attitudes or deeds.

These restrictive rules are indoctrinated in us by the people who care for us as we are growing up. They become part of the code of ethics by which we regulate thoughts and behaviors. These rules of conduct that are so early and deeply embedded in us, and that are the products of our rearing even before we are able to talk—and, for some of us, for some years thereafter—form our unconscious conscience (superego). Most of us do not know the extent and force of this very restrictive, self-punitive portion of our conscience. Our conscious conscience (ego ideal) also contains restrictive and inhibiting forces (negative ego ideal), but our positive goals and aspirations can be classified as belonging to our ego ideal. Our unconscious conscience sets limits on how honestly and directly we can let ourselves see some of the more unacceptable drives in our dreams. This process of self-constraint against freely discovering and understanding ourselves has been called "resistance" by psychoanalysts.

The clues that our unconscious conscience is at work, setting limits on how far we can proceed with continuing self-analysis of dreams, are usually not conscious thoughts that we should resist, or that we are doing something evil or unforgivable. Rather, the clues are likely to be moodiness, depression, growing lack of interest in the pursuit, or perhaps a sense of fatigue, or an idea that the whole enterprise is foolish or mystical and without validity. These are a few of the ways in which the unconscious deterrents to learning about oneself are manifested. Another, more difficult clue to deal with is that one may begin not to remember one's dreams, which obviously brings the whole enterprise to a decisive halt.

Sometimes, some self-scrutiny into the strict, forbidden areas that are part of one's code of behavior helps change the strength of this resistance. Or a self-reminder that thoughts and feelings are much different, in actuality and in their consequences, from actions and deeds may lessen this resistance. (For example, the wish for someone to drop dead is legally and actually much different from the actuality, and everyone has had such ideas in a lifetime, with varying amounts of guilt and self-recrimination, of course.) Sometimes telling the dream to someone else, someone who can be trusted and who is interested in self-knowledge and dream analysis, will provide some leads about the inhibiting and constraining motivations in the dream, and hence in the dreamer. This other person may see the dream with a fresh viewpoint and be able to point out to us the self-punitive and self-restrictive aspects of the dream. For most of us, our unacceptable impulses toward others are accompanied by equally unkind impulses toward ourselves. Running away from self-realization of these urges in our dreams does not change us in any way; we will still behave in the same ways toward others and ourselves. Delving into more self-understanding through our dreams, though this will not dramatically cure us of psychological conflicts bred in childhood, will move us in the direction of knowing ourselves better. I do not want to leave the reader with the impression that it is always safe and wise to turn to another person who has an amateur interest in dream analysis, and to enlist this person in seriously analyzing and interpreting one's dreams. Truly expert assistance from others in such a project requires long and ethical professional training. The services of a psychoanalytically trained therapist are the most effective measure toward eliminating blocks in self-analysis of one's dreams.

2. Even though a dreamer is not blocked by an unconscious conscience (which dictates that knowing too much about oneself is dangerous), the dreamer lacks the knowledge about and experience with dreams that makes this approach easy or fruitful.

Some people have a knack for self-inquiry and are quite psychologically minded about themselves. Such people can make use of the ideas presented here and learn more about themselves. On the other hand, some people are not very psychologically minded though they may be brilliant in their vocations, whether in the business world, engineering, and the sciences, or the legal or medical professions. They tend to relate to others in terms of surface reactions or external appearances and are not inclined to look for underlying causes, to ask why a person said or did such and such a thing. They tend to relate to their own selves in the same manner. Many individuals of this sort can improve their skills in understanding their own psychology. But many cannot. And they cannot be expected to make much headway in analyzing their own dreams, including a single dream.

Even people who are highly motivated and psychologically minded may run into problems on dream analysis. They may have difficulty in free-associating on dream details or on the dream as a whole. They may also want to conclude that the dream stimulus was some trivial current event rather than an event which meant more to them than they had previously realized, an event that mobilized some deeper psychological issues that had been silent — or an event that reminded them of some distantly related psychological matters with which they were struggling.

With firm determination to know oneself, one can overcome many of these obstacles and make steady progress through dream analysis toward enlightening glimpses of oneself. Through regular contact with this facet of one's mental processes, dream analysis can contribute to a better appreciation of one's identity and potentiality and can provide a sense of relative stability and familiarity to the great diversity of unpredictable, confusing thoughts and feelings that may bombard our mental life.

INTEGRATING THE RESULTS OF SELF-ANALYSIS TO REMEDY ONE'S PROBLEMS

Using the processes of introspection, self-scrutiny, free association, and dream analysis, you can make considerable headway toward understanding the childhood origins of most of your emotional conflicts, and the life experiences that have tended to reinforce them. You should be able to figure out which experiences originally caused the anxieties or depressions or other problems involving your self-esteem; and you should know whether these problems amount to underevaluation or overevaluation of your self. You should try to think about and understand the defenses and coping methods that began to develop at the time in your life that these conflicts and stresses originated. It would then be wise to try to determine whether or not there might be better methods of coping with the daily reminders of these stresses and the various resulting conflicts.

The main methods that professional therapists use, after discerning what originally caused our emotional problems, are aimed at helping us explore new ways of coping with the adverse behaviors and feelings we have learned. Many skillful therapists recommend at this point in psychotherapy that the patient assume the psychological position of "risk-taking," which does not mean participating in some foolish or indiscriminate actions. Rather, with this approach the therapist tries to get the patient to have the courage to attempt to do things or to feel emotions that he or she was previously inhibited from doing or feeling. Another approach that good therapists use is to try to get the patient to explore and develop better and more mature ways of coping with situations that are or have been worrisome, discouraging, or frightening. These are some of the basic ways in which good therapists help us not only to understand the origins of our problems, but also to get a handle on finding more effective ways of dealing with them.

When one has a professional psychotherapist, instead of oneself, the psychotherapist helps to put together the facts turned up by introspection, free association, and dream analysis, and tries to explain how these facts relate to our problems — how they clarify, for example, development of a psychoneurosis or some kind of behavior disorder such as drug or alcohol abuse. Without an external psychotherapist, you yourself have to do this job of integrating and clarifying the information obtained from free association and dream analysis in such a way that it is possible to understand how you happened to develop the problems on which you are working.

There are two very important factors that can slow a person down and inhibit progress during the course of such self-analysis. These two factors are (1) adverse countertransference attitudes and (2) persisting feelings of hopelessness and helplessness. Let us consider these two factors consecutively.

COUNTERTRANSFERENCE DIFFICULTIES IN SELF-ANALYSIS

Usually the word "countertransference" signifies attitudes and feelings that a psychotherapist experiences toward the patient, feelings that were previously evoked by significant persons in the therapists's lifetime. Countertransference was discovered by psychoanalysts to be an important factor in determining whether or not psychoanalysis was successful. Psychoanalysts found that adverse and negative feelings and memories aroused in the analyst by the free-associative material brought up by the patient could often lead to the therapist's developing negative attitudes toward the patient, such that the analyst might, consciously or unconsciously, become unable to be of psychotherapeutic benefit to this patient. Psychoanalysts therefore decided that it was essential for every psychoanalytic trainee to first undergo his or her own analysis, so that there might be not only a resolution and an improvement in understanding of any childhood neuroses, but that the unconscious would be made conscious. In other words, through a personal psychoanalysis with a training analyst the analytic trainee developed a greater awareness about what made him tick, and thus his right hand understood better what his left hand was inclined to do. The fact that trained psychoanalysts have had their own emotional quirks dealt with so that they are less likely to stumble over their own feet is one important reason why such a person is often to be preferred as a therapist. Naturally, this criterion sets some limitations on what an untrained psychotherapist can achieve through working on his or her own self. But remember, Sigmund Freud did psychoanalyze himself and made great progress in understanding and overcoming some of his problems. Moreover, there is no reason why one cannot, from time to time, obtain some external supervision in order to get an objective check on the validity of one's self-analysis, just as a well-qualified psychotherapist or psychoanalyst does from time to time.

Most psychoanalysts include the conscious attitudes and feelings of the therapist toward a patient as part of what is called "countertransference." Such conscious feelings are not automatically and uniformly benign from the mental health point of view when the therapist is oneself. For example, a person may have either a consciously hateful idea of the self or an overvalued self-appraisal. That is, some individuals consciously hate themselves and despise their own efforts; whereas others have exaggerated ideas of their self-importance to the point of demanding extraordinary self-entitlement and rewards. These extreme self-views are almost always markers of some degree of mental illness. When such viewpoints are encountered in oneself, it is wise to try to hold them in abeyance rather than to act on them. Self-analysis and self-psychotherapy can uncover the origins of such extreme points of view, and can, potentially, help one obtain a more level-headed perspective about the relative values of one's self.

During the process of self-analysis, if one discovers that an extreme point of view of this sort is operative in one's free associations and dream analysis, one should try to discover what has caused such a viewpoint rather than blandly accepting it. Also, strong hateful impulses or inordinate loving impulses toward others are signs of adverse countertransferences. Such extreme points of view should be looked upon as signs or symptoms of one's neurotic personality rather than a perspective that is completely normal and valid.

There are some religions and philosophical systems that espouse and encourage extreme feelings of self-love or self-hate and/or the love or hate of others. Moreover, in times of stress all of us can become vulnerable to such feelings. It is wise to question whether such an arousal of strong feelings is coming from a cult that is trying to influence one's mind and behavior for the purposes of exploitation by others. Most religious and philosophical points of view are entirely consistent with accepted criteria of mental health, but there are some that are not. Hence, conscious attitudes of strong over- or under-appraisal of the value of the self or others should be looked upon with some suspicion and as manifestations of negative mental health that need understanding, clarification, and remedying. Either of these extreme feelings could stem from a psychological state that developed at some earlier time in our life, as a result of circumstances generating from the people and situations around us at the time. But out of their original context, such self-attitudes may be archaic and outdated.

What about *unconscious* countertransference attitudes and feelings? Psychoanalysts have a number of ways of discovering these. Since psychoanalysts have gone through their own personal psychoanalysis, they have some awareness of how they got to be the persons they are. They usually have some accurate sense of which times and situations in their lives have been suppressed and repressed in their memories. Moreover, psychoanalysts continually do self-analysis in their practices and in their private lives. Self-analysis becomes a way of life. They continually let themselves free-associate in response to what their patients say or do, and even explore whether their own dreams throw any light upon their more obscure reactions to their patients. This gives them insights into unconscious reactions to the material their patients present to them. They then use such subjective reactions to help clarify their own attitudes, evoked by the arousal of past memories, to their patients.

When doing self-analysis one obviously has to do this job oneself. Can it be done without stumbling over oneself? Yes. But it is necessary to keep alert and to remember that some of the past experiences one is digging up may well be accompanied by childhood or young adulthood attitudes that were prevalent at the time of those experiences — and that those attitudes may or may not be outdated or otherwise inappropriate. If one can pin down which such countertransference attitudes — based on experiences just recently brought into conscious memory — are outdated or inappropriate, one can clear the way toward more successful self-analysis.

Psychoanalysts themselves have difficulties in validly assessing their countertransference, according to the proceedings of a scientific panel held at the 1984 meeting of the American Psychoanalytic Association (Renik 1986). The writer states, based on this panel, that the function of analysis of countertransference is to achieve "analytic neutrality" in spite of the "imperfection of psychoanalytic methodology." He asserts that various analytic observers do "gain relatively objective data" and can reach consensus, but that countertransference should not be substituted for empathy and understanding (p. 706).

Renik observes also that psychoanalysts are constantly influenced by feelings from their personal lives and that they are consciously aware of only a fraction of this influence regardless of how experienced, talented, and conscientious they are. This limits the analyst's conceptualization of the psychoanalytic process, places the analyst in the position of making mistakes without realizing it, and may result in the analyst doing useful things for reasons not entirely understood. Renik reflects, hopefully, that the clinical reports by panel members of their recognition of countertransference problems may possibly be a precursor to insight for both the analyst and analysand (p. 707).

HOPELESSNESS AND HELPLESSNESS AS HINDRANCES TO SELF-ANALYSIS

Attitudes of hopelessness and helplessness can be so oppressive and pervasive that one has no energy or motivation to do self-analysis of any kind. On the other hand, a regularly and consistently hopeful attitude about one's purpose in life and one's existence and ability to succeed will tend to ensure success in one's self-analysis. If it is possible for one to adopt a hopeful attitude about the prospect of success in any endeavor, there is good scientific evidence, as a matter of fact, that one is more likely to achieve such success.

What if there are overpowering feelings of hopelessness and helplessness? If one cannot overcome such feelings through will power, or through continued attempts to understand and remedy such markers of poor mental health, successful self-analysis is very difficult to achieve. Overpowering hopelessness and helplessness may be a sign that one should seek professional outside help. A professional therapist, under such circumstances, is more inclined to see the situation objectively and consider whether psychoactive antidepressant drugs might be useful. In addition, a professional is better able to assess which kind of psychotherapeutic help would be most effective.

THE PSYCHOANALYTIC APPROACH TO EXISTENTIAL ISSUES

The life problem that one wants to get help with may involve, primarily, issues about the purpose of one's existence and the nature of one's identity. No one type of psychotherapy has the simplest or best answer to such broad issues. Most religions and philosophical theories deal with the purpose of life and the issue of life after death. They do not necessarily, however, deal with the changes in one's identity throughout the life cycle.

For any approach to be successful, it is necessary to keep continually in mind the problems one wants to solve with respect to existence and/or personal identity. After doing so, one must realize that different psychotherapeutic approaches have somewhat different theories about existence and identity.

The psychoanalytic approach does not attempt to offer a cosmic view of the universe nor any speculation concerning immortal life. On the other hand, psychoanalysis does not attempt to negate any world views, since it claims no expertise or special enlightenment in these areas. It does, however, propose certain purposes for human existence; for example, it holds that the purpose of life is to love and to work, and that mental health is associated with the capacity to perform well in both of these arenas. Psychoanalysis makes no pronouncements about the presence or absence of God(s), leaving such beliefs open to the preferences of each individual. Hence, a psychoanalyst cannot be expected to have any special knowledge with regard to such questions. On the other hand, psychoanalysts agree that the articulation and clarification of these beliefs are appropriate goals for each individual. An individual's ideals and life goals, as well as his or her emotions, though not generally labeled by psychoanalysis as "spiritual" matters, are regarded as the biopsychosocial and cultural consequences of one's upbringing. These are all regarded as appropriate areas for self-scrutiny, self-insight, and self-revelation. The acquiring of a neurotic or a psychotic point of view in one's system of, for example, religious or philosophical beliefs, is a legitimate subject for psychoanalytic investigation. For example, the concept of a God being merciless and unforgiving would be considered by a psychoanalyst as a neurotic consequence of a child's having had a harsh and unforgiving parent, especially if the individual's formal religion does not propose such a concept of God. Hence, psychoanalytically oriented self-analysis will tend to focus on the irrational components of one's secular and philosophical belief system, and how these might have been influenced by personal experiences in one's formative years. Psychoanalytic self-analysis, since it evolved from Western culture, and specifically from Europe, is imbued with Judeo–Christian ethics and ideals. Some other religious orientations, however, have incorporated psychoanalytic ideas with respect to the influence of unconscious motivations and behavior and the effects of childhood experiences in shaping adult behavior. The Moslem, Hindu, and Buddhist religions have interfaced with psychoanalytic approaches.

Psychoanalysis has been particularly interested in identifying the changes in the self or in one's identity during different stages of the life cycle. Psychoanalysts recommend continuing analysis or self-analysis during different stages of the life cycle in order to help the individual reassess and reshape his or her identity to fit each stage of life. In fact, an important part of a person's psychoanalysis usually involves learning about the appropriateness of one's conscious identity with respect to one's present stage of life. To some extent, significant headway can also be made on such a project through the use of self-analysis.

A BRIEF EXAMPLE OF A SUCCESSFUL SELF-ANALYSIS AND FURTHER COMMENTS ON OBSTACLES THAT MAY BE ENCOUNTERED

Farrow (1945) after 200 hours of analysis under two different systems of psychotherapy, decided to analyze himself. He adopted Freud's method of analyzing his dreams — including writing down everything that came to his mind from various periods of his life. He found that he was able to recreate emotional experiences of life events that had occurred as early as 6 months of age. Following these reconstructions and remembrances, he experienced an improvement in his health and sense of well-being.

Horney (1942) has discussed various obstacles often encountered in self-analysis, including the problem of maintaining strong motivation without an external psychotherapist, and the possibility of stopping too soon with self-analysis after removing a few difficulties and then arranging your life to fit the unresolved portion of your neurosis. She also warned that in self-therapy you might not find it easy to deal with the problems you uncover.

In this book, many suggestions have been made on recognizing and trying to deal with some of these blocks to successful self-psychotherapy. It must be acknowledged that some people, such as psychotics, do not even recognize that they need psychotherapy, no matter how obvious their mental and emotional predicament might be to others. Others might well be aware that they have a problem, but be unable to interpret its nature. For example, an individual suffering from a psychosomatic disorder (in which an emotional problem causes a physiological one), such as bronchial asthma or colitis, or a so-called hysterical conversion symptom (in which there is no biological basis for the disability), such as tubular vision or glove-like loss of sensation in the hand, would realize there is something wrong; however, he or she would attribute the symptoms to physical causes and be unaware that they stemmed from psychological ones. To suggest some kind of self-psychotherapy to such a person might be perceived as inappropriate.

4

The Meditative Approach

APPLYING MEDITATION
TO EXISTENTIAL ISSUES

Meditative approaches to existential matters may coincide with some aspects of the psychoanalytic approach. However, they generally focus more on different levels of consciousness. Some proponents of meditation emphasize that it will help one achieve higher states of consciousness in which it is possible to detach oneself from earthly preoccupations. As we move from psychoanalytic self-scrutiny to meditative methods and religious approaches in seeking solutions to existential problems, we tend to refer to subjective experiences and fantasies in "spiritual" terms. Some meditative approaches thus make use of the designation of a "soul" or "spirit" within each individual, and imbue this with an existence of its own, separate from the body in which it ordinarily resides. Some approaches go so far as to claim that there is a separate existence to this spirit or soul, which can be reincarnated in different bodies, human or nonhuman, over countless years. None of these beliefs have scientific or empirical substance, as the scientific method has no means to support or refute such beliefs. For individuals who seriously entertain such beliefs, however, some meditative approaches may be worth using.

A word of caution may be appropriate here, for a line needs to be drawn between the real and the non-real world. So long as these two domains can be recognized and differentiated, there probably is no serious problem. There is a normal human need for wish-fulfillment; however, the inability to discriminate between the real and unreal world or between fact and fiction characterizes mental illness — that is, psychosis or insanity. In our wish-fulfilling daydreams or immediately after our night dreams, we customarily have to make these distinctions. That is, we have to distinguish between our fantasy life, based upon the marvelous or scary fictions we can invent, and the sometimes disappointing dimensions of the everyday world. A mentally healthy individual can venture into either domain, can even develop some excellent ideas from the fantasy world and then effectively apply them to the real world and more or less continually be able to make a distinction between fact and fantasy. But since many meditative practices are designed to take one away from the real world, the practicing of a return to reality should be a regular exercise for the individual using meditative approaches. Also, most of the time the goals of meditative approaches will help an individual primarily with understanding the various levels of consciousness that can be achieved, rather than providing a means to get direct solutions to the problems of everyday living.

LEARNING HOW TO MEDITATE

The main goal of meditation is to make contact with your inner mental processes and to allow yourself to retreat from your busy mind. Ordinarily your mind is filled with many sensory impressions, thoughts, and feelings. Instead of trying to make sense of these things and place them into chronological sequence, one tries through meditation to achieve special enlightenment through turning off this steady flow of outer and inner stimuli.

One simple exercise originating from Zen Buddhism emphasizes breathing as a physiological catalyst to achieve a state of relaxation. To begin, you are encouraged to find a quiet place free from distractions. Try to select a place and time that you can use regularly for your daily meditation so that it becomes a habit. Experts advise not choosing a time immediately after a meal. Having located a place, sit quietly in a chair which provides support for your back and shut your eyes.

Take an inventory of your body, noting any tensions or discomforts. If you find some tensions, breathe in and then, on exhalation, gently relax your muscles as much as you can. When you have finished your physical evaluation, carry out a mental and emotional inventory. When you find any source of anxiety or discomfort, let yourself feel it momentarily, and then gently erase it from your mind. Instead of trying to force away the anxious ideas, allow these ideas to drain out of your awareness by focusing your attention somewhere else.

In time you will become relaxed both physically and mentally. Now let yourself become conscious of your breathing. When you become aware of thoughts that are inclined to take your attention away from your breathing, let the thoughts come, but continue to turn your attention to your breathing. You cannot expect your mind to be completely focused on your respiration. Your mind will wander away from it many times. You are, nevertheless, meditating even though your mind does wander. The meditation process involves bringing your mind back, time and again, to your respiration, until being able to focus your attention becomes habitual.

As an alternative to focusing on your breathing, you may want to try visualizing your breathing by imagining your breath as vapor that you can see flowing into your nose or your mouth and down into your throat, into your lungs and even through your body. You can imagine the vapor flowing deep into your abdomen, and then the vapor rising and going out of your body as you exhale. You can see the vapor disappear into the air. Then you can begin the process of imagining inhaling the vapor all over again.

Another alternative is to count your breaths. You

can count your inhalation as "one," and your exhalation and your next inhalation as "two," and so on.

As you concentrate on your respiration — whether by direct focusing or by visualization, counting, or any other means — do not try to change or control it in any way. Rather, let your breathing regulate itself spontaneously, which it does anyway if you let it do so.

You should be prepared to stop this exercise after ten to twenty minutes. Simply stop concentrating on your breathing. Doing so will return you to your normal level of consciousness. Blink your eyes a few times, then open them and sit silently for a minute or so. When you arise, you will feel refreshed and relaxed.

AN EXAMPLE OF SUBJECTIVE EXPERIENCES DURING TWO YEARS OF INSIGHT MEDITATION

Walsh (1984), a professor of psychiatry and a neuroscientist, has described the first two years of his own meditative experiences, in an attempt to provide a sense of the powerful and personally meaningful nature of the procedure. The account of his experiences is quoted in detail here to give you an impression of what subjective experiences may be in store for those among you who are considering trying meditation.

> This is an account of the subjective experiences of some
> 2 years of Vipassana or Insight meditation. During the
> first year this comprised an average of approximately 1

hour per day. During the second year this was increased to about 2 hours, as well as some 6 weeks of intensive meditation retreats, usually of 2 weeks duration. These retreats comprised about 18 to 20 hours daily of continuous walking and sitting meditation performed in total silence and without eye contact, reading or writing. While this amount of practice may be vastly less than that of more experienced practitioners, it has certainly proved sufficient to elicit a range of experiences beyond the ken of day-to-day nonmeditative living.

I began meditation with one-half hour each day and during the first 3–6 months there were few times during which I could honestly say with compete certainty that I was definitely experiencing benefits from it. Except for the painfully obvious stiff back and sore knees, the psychological effects other than occasional relaxation felt so subtle and ephemeral that I could never be sure that they were more than a figment of my wishes and expectations. The nature of meditation seems to be, especially at first, a slow but cumulative process, a fact which may be useful for beginners to be aware of.

However, with continued perseverance subtle effects just at the limit of my perceptual threshold began to become apparent. I had expected the eruption into awareness of powerful, concrete experiences, if not flashes of lightning and pealing of bells, then at least something of sufficient intensity to make it very clear that I had "gotten it," what "it" was. What "it" actually turned out to be was not the appearance of formerly nonexistent mental phenomena, but rather a gradual incremental increase in perceptual sensitivity to the formerly subliminal portions of my own inner stream of consciousness.

When one sits down with eyes closed to silence the mind,
one is at first submerged by a torrent of thoughts. . . .
The more sensitive I became, the more I was forced to
recognize that what I had formerly believed to be my
rational mind preoccupied with cognition, planning,
problem solving, etc., actually comprised a frantic torrent of forceful, demanding, loud, and often unrelated
thoughts and fantasies which filled an unbelievable proportion of consciousness even during purposive behavior. The incredible proportion of consciousness which
this fantasy world occupied, my powerlessness to remove it for more than a few seconds, and my former
state of mindlessness or ignorance of its existence stag-
gered me. Interestingly, this mindlessness seemed much
more intense and difficult to deal with than in psychotherapy, when the depth and sensitivity of inner awareness seemed less, and where the therapist provided a
perceptual focus and was available to pull me back if I
started to get lost in fantasy.

The subtlety, complexity, infinite range and number,
and entrapping power of the fantasies which the mind
creates seems impossible to comprehend, to differentiate from reality while in them and even more so to
describe to one who has not experienced them. Layer
upon layer of imagery and quasilogic open up at any
point to which attention is directed. Indeed, it gradually becomes apparent it is impossible to question and
reason one's way out of this all-encompassing fantasy
since the very process of questioning, thinking, and
seeking only creates further fantasy.

The power and pervasiveness of these inner dialogues
and fantasies left me amazed that we could be so
unaware of them during our normal waking life and
reminded me of the Eastern concept of maya, of
all-consuming illusion.

The First Meditation Retreat

The first meditation retreat, begun about 1 year after commencing sitting, was a very painful and difficult 2-week affair. A marked hypersensitivity to all stimuli both internal and external rapidly developed, resulting in intense arousal, agitation, discomfort, and multiple chronic muscle contractions, especially around the shoulders.

One of the most amazing rediscoveries during this first retreat was the incredible proportion of time, well over 90%, which I spent lost in fantasy. Most of these were of the ego self-aggrandizing type, so that when eventually I realized I was in them, it proved quite a struggle to decide to give them up and return to the breath, but with practice this decision became slightly easier, faster, and more automatic. This by no means happened quickly since over the first 4 or 5 days the proportion of time spent in fantasy actually increased as the meditation deepened. During this period, each time I sat and closed my eyes I would be immediately swept away by vivid hallucinations, losing all contact with where I was or what I was doing until after an unknown period of time a thought would creep in such as "Am I really swimming, lying on the beach?" etc., and then I would either get lost back into the fantasy or another thought would come: "Wait a moment, I thought I was meditating." If the latter, then I would be left with the difficult problem of trying to ground myself, i.e., of differentiating between stimulus-produced precepts ("reality") and entirely endogenous ones ("hallucinations"). The only way this seemed possible was to try finding the breath, and so I would begin frantically searching around in this hypnagogic universe for the sensations of the breath. Such was the power of the hallucinations that sometimes I would be literally unable to find it and would fall back into the fantasy. If successful, I would recognize it and be reassured that I was in fact meditating. Then in the next moment I would be lost again in yet another fantasy. The clarity, power, persuasiveness, and continuity of these hallucinations is difficult to express adequately. However, the effect of living through 3 days during which time to close my eyes meant losing contact almost immediately with ordinary reality was extraordinarily draining, to say the least. Interestingly enough while this experience was uncomfortable and quite beyond my control, it was not particularly frightening; if anything the opposite was true. For many years I had feared losing control if I let down defenses and voyaged too far along the road of self-investigation and discovery. This appears to be [a] common fear in most growth traditions and seems to serve a major defensive function. Having experienced this once-feared outcome, it now no longer seems so terrifying. Of course, the paradox is that what we usually call control is actually exactly the opposite, a lack of ability to let go of defenses.

While a good 90% or more of this first retreat was taken up with mindless fantasy and agitation, there did occur during the second week occasional short-lived periods of intense peace and tranquility. These were so satisfying that, while I would not be willing to sign up for a life-time in a monastery, I could begin to comprehend the possibility of the truth of the Buddhist saying that "peace is the highest form of happiness." Affective lability was also extreme. There were not infrequently sudden apparently unprecipitated wide mood swings to completely polar emotions. Shorn of all my props and distractions, it became clear that I had little more than the faintest inkling of self-control over either thoughts or feelings and that my mind had a mind of its own.

It soon became apparent that the type of material which forcibly erupted into awareness and disrupted concentration was most often material — ideas, fantasies, thoughts, etc. — to which I was attached (addicted) and around which there was considerable affective charge. There was a definite sense that attachments reduced the flexibility and power of the mind, since whenever I was preoccupied with a stimulus to which I was attached, then I had difficulty in withdrawing my attention from it to observe other stimuli which passed through awareness.

Paradoxically it seems that a need or attachment to be rid of certain experience or state may lead to its perpetuation. The clearest example of this has been with anxiety. Some months ago I suddenly began to experience mild anxiety attacks of unknown origin which, curiously enough, seemed to occur most often when I was feeling really good and in the presence of a particular person whom I loved. At such times I would try all my various psychological gymnastics to eradicate it since it was clearly not okay with me to feel anxious. However, these episodes continued for some 5 months in spite of, or as it actually turned out because of, my resistance to them. During this time my practice deepened and I was able to examine more and more of the process during meditation. What I found was that I had considerable fear of fear and my mind therefore surveyed in a radarlike fashion all endogenous and exogenous stimuli for their fear-evoking potential, and all reactions for any fear component. Thus there was a continuous mental radarlike scanning process present in an exquisitely sensitive fashion for the detection of anything resembling fear. Consequently, there were a considerable number of false positive, i.e., non-fearful stimuli and reactions which were interpreted as being fearful or potentially fear-provoking.

Since the reactions to the false positives themselves comprised fear and fear components, there was, of

course, an immediate chain reaction set up with one
fear response acting as the stimulus for the next. It
thus became very clear that my fear of, and resistance
to, fear was exactly what was perpetuating it.

This insight and the further application of meditative
awareness to the process certainly reduced but did not
eradicate these episodes entirely. Paradoxically they
still tended to recur when I felt very calm and peaceful.
It was not until the middle of the next meditation
retreat that the reasons for this became clear. After the
first few days of pain and agitation I began to feel
more and more peaceful and there came a sitting in
which I could feel my meditation deepen perceptibly
and the restless mental scanning slow more and more.
Then as the process continued to deepen and slow, I
was literally jolted by a flash of agitation and anxiety
accompanying a thought—"But what do I do now if
there's no more anxiety to look for?" It was apparent
that if I continued to quieten, there would be neither
anxiety to scan for nor a scanning process itself, and
my need to get rid of anxiety demanded that I have a
continuous scanning mechanism, and the presence of
the mechanism, in turn, created the presence of anxiety. My "but what do I do now?" fear had very
effectively removed the possibility of the dissipation of
both, and its occurrence at a time when I was feeling
most peaceful, relaxed and safe, of course explained
why I had been subject to these anxiety episodes at the
apparently paradoxical times when I felt best. Paradoxically then it appears that within the mind, if you
need to be rid of certain experiences, then not only are
you likely to experience a number of false positives but
you may also need to have them around continuously
so you can keep getting rid of them. Thus within the
province of the mind, what you resist is what you get.

With continued practice the speed, power, loudness,
and continuity of thoughts and fantasies began to

slowly diminish, leaving subtle sensations of greater peace and quiet. After a period of about 4 or 5 months there occurred episodes in which I would open my eyes at the end of meditation and look at the outside world without the presence of concomitant internal dialogue. This state would be rapidly terminated by a rising sense of anxiety and anomie accompanied by the thought, "I don't know what anything means." Thus, I could be looking at something completely familiar, such as a tree, a building, or the sky, and yet without an accompanying internal dialogue to label and categorize it, it felt totally strange and devoid of meaning. [pp. 265–267]

In his report, Walsh goes on to tell that as he continued to practice meditation, he experienced greater peace and quiet and perceptual sensitivity. And these experiences led him to a greater understanding of and willingness to surrender to the meditative process.

5

Behavior and Conditioning

Self-Psychotherapy

SYSTEMATIC DESENSITIZATION

Systematic desensitization involves taking a fear or anxiety that you have, and imagining it while you are in a state of deep relaxation. The theory behind this approach is that if you are comfortable and relaxed, the anxious feelings that customarily occur in association with a stressful event will begin to lessen, and then will eventually disappear.

To pinpoint the range and magnitude of your fears it is useful to list them. In doing so, write down the situations which are most fear-arousing and those that are least so; list these events in decreasing order of their capacity to elicit your anxiety.

Now put yourself in a state of relaxation, following the instructions that have been previously given. Once you are relaxed, imagine the least fear-arousing item on the list (for example, "I am invited to introduce myself to a group of strangers"). If you become aware of some apprehension at the thought of this, stop the scene and relax yourself again. Once you are aware of having no tension when you evoke the mental imagery of a certain situation, proceed to the next-higher anxiety-arousing situation on your list. Continue stepwise in the above manner until you can visualize all situations on your list with no anxiety. You should practice this daily for about thirty minutes. Of course, if you find yourself dealing with very severe anxiety or panic you should try a different method or consider seeking professional help.

BEHAVIORAL PROGRAMMING

Behavioral programming involves the ways in which you deal with yourself after you reach a goal that you or someone else set for you. Do you reward yourself (mentally, verbally, imaginatively, materially)? Or do you punish yourself (mentally, verbally, imaginatively, materially)? That is, do you give yourself a reward—a verbal caress, the imagined congratulations of others, some food, or something purchased? Or do you punish yourself and tell yourself that you could have done better or deprive yourself of some material thing? And if you do not meet the goals you have set, how do you deal with yourself—are you tolerant, forgiving, punishing?

Behaviorists believe that we all maintain a constant inner dialogue or monologue, rewarding or punishing ourselves and/or others. These theorists hold that there are three ways by which we learn: *classical conditioning, operant conditioning,* and *modeling.* Classical conditioning involves the pairing or association of one stimulus with another, as in systematic desensitization. Operant conditioning involves the relationship between a behavior and its consequences; that is, does one follow the behavior with a reward or a punishment or no response? Modeling refers to learning by observing the behavior of others, as in learning from the examples set by others how to play a musical instrument or to do public speaking or to behave like a woman in our culture. Obtaining a reward increases the likelihood that one will behave in that way again. Receiving a punishment decreases that likelihood. So if you do someone a favor and this behavior elicits an adverse criticism, you are less likely to do another favor for this person.

SELF-REINFORCEMENT (SELF-REWARDING VERSUS SELF-PUNISHING)

Behavior and conditioning therapists recommend self-reinforcement as a method of improving a person's self-esteem and decreasing feelings of shame and guilt associated with mental depression. To use this method you are instructed to list five things that you might say to yourself that would make you feel good. Examples of these might be: I feel proud of how much progress I am making in my self-change project; I feel good that I got a B + in that algebra test; I am a great son; I am truly lovable; I have a nice body. Because many of us are reared with the idea that we should not praise ourselves and that modesty is more to be rewarded than pride, you might find it difficult to list positive statements about yourself. Individuals with a neurotic depression often have problems in this area, for they suffer irrational self-criticism possibly based on harsh parental criticism, early-childhood parental loss, or other life events that have undermined their self-evaluation. They have a deficiency of self-love or narcissism rather than too much. Such individuals need encouragement and even insistence from their therapists—themselves, in this case—to list five positive personal characteristics. Nevertheless, their reservations and resistance must be noted in order to get a sound idea of how arbitrary and strict a conscience and self-appraisal they have.

After you have completed the list of positive statements that you can make about yourself, now please think about and list five things or events that make you feel good (such as eating fruits, solving problems, listening to music, playing with pet animals, being praised, making somebody happy, and so on).

Now you are advised to consider how often during a week you do the things that make you feel good. And how often do you say things to yourself that make you feel good? Whatever number you might come up with, now try to increase how often you say things to yourself that make you feel good and do things that make you feel good. In the behavioral approach, an effort is made to precisely consider the nature and content of your thoughts as well as their order in a sequence; that is, do they represent antecedents to actions, consequences of actions, or actions themselves? By paying attention to such details, behaviorists believe you can put yourself in a position to determine the most constructive use of thoughts and images to reach your own specific goals. For instance, you might use these private images and statements to help you learn to perform certain behaviors better, to increase your self-esteem, to initiate some kind of action, to interrupt maladaptive behavior, or to increase your motivation to succeed.

SUBJECTIVE IMAGES AND SELF-STATEMENTS AS BEHAVIORAL REHEARSALS

Evoking subjective images and internalized statements may provide a means of practicing or rehearsing for actual future behaviors. There is evidence that practicing an event facilitates actually performing the action. Such images may be used, also, to make a psychomotor task like hitting a tennis or golf ball easier and more successful. A study with student basketball players showed a positive relationship between subjective imagery and successful action. A group of students was randomly divided into three groups. Each group took a pre-test of how many free throws they could make. The first group practiced free throws for a certain amount of time each day for twenty days, and then took a post-test on day twenty. The second group did no practice and took a post-test on day twenty. The third group imagined making free throws during the twenty days, and if they missed a shot in their imagination, they imagined themselves correcting the mistake; on day twenty this group, also, took a post-test. Group two showed no improvement in twenty days, group one showed 24 percent improvement, and group three (practicing only in their imaginations) improved 23 percent!

SUBJECTIVE IMAGES AND SELF-STATEMENTS AS MEANS OF STRESS AND TENSION REDUCTION

In classical systematic desensitization, relaxation preceded the fear-arousing imagery. In another approach, the fear-arousing situation becomes a cue for relaxation. In this method, you let your self notice anxiety by imagining the fear-arousing situation and maintaining that situation in your imagination. Now, while maintaining the tension, you practice controlling and reducing your anxiety by means of muscular relaxation and self-modeling (that is, you observe your self acting in a competent and successful fashion in the fear-arousing situation). You also employ self-instructions to cope better with the situation (for example, thinking about being in control and being able to handle the situation).

Try taking a moment to recall a situation in which you felt anxious in the past or one in which you anticipate feeling anxious in the future. Go through the situation in your mind and let yourself experience the feelings that occur. Now, holding the image in your mind, focus on your breathing, and give yourself instructions to relax. Keep the image of the situation in your mind and practice acting in that situation as you might like to act. Let your imagination portray you acting in exactly the way you would like to. Experiment with different self-instructions that seem most appropriate to you. Using this procedure will tend to bring about changes in feelings and actions in the direction you desire.

SUBJECTIVE SELF-STATEMENTS DEALING WITH CAUSALITY

When an event occurs, how do you evaluate the cause of that event? Was the event good or bad? Was the event outside your control, or did you play a part in its occurrence?

It will be helpful to you to observe for a week or month the kinds of subjective self-statements that you make. On doing so, you will want to assess which statements are in your own best interests and which are not. You can now make a list of positive self-statements. Keep this list accessible and practice instructing yourself to increase the frequency of these kinds of positive statements. On doing so you will notice that your self-evaluation and self-esteem will gradually and definitely improve. If these features of your self-appraisal do not change in a favorable direction, consider using a different method of self-psychotherapy. Or you might think of seeking the opinion and advice of a professional therapist.

THE USE OF MEDITATION COMBINED WITH BEHAVIORAL AND CONDITIONING SELF-PSYCHOTHERAPY

Shapiro (1978) has described the combined use of meditation and behavioral self-psychotherapy to overcome low self-esteem. His patient was a woman in her middle forties who often felt on the verge of becoming an alcoholic because of her binge drinking. She would spend many hours of the day planning what she was going to do, but whenever she decided to carry out these plans she would pull back from fear of failure. This avoidance behavior involved a wide variety of activities, such as avoiding job-hunting and avoiding meeting new people, and even routine behaviors such as avoiding taking a shower or brushing her teeth. After accumulating a large number of failed performances, she would become ashamed of her lack of accomplishments and would experience a need to make up for lost time by performing one great and important action. She would first go on a drinking spree to prepare for living out some unrealistic fantasy.

This woman observed that she never gave herself the opportunity to have any pleasure, for if she tried to do so she would feel guilty for wasting her time in so doing rather than accomplishing something worthwhile. In other words, she allayed her guilt over nonachievement by bribing her conscience through her obsession with accomplishing important things and her refusal to allow herself any fun. Hence, she spent most of her time putting herself down, telling herself she was worthless and unlovable.

Her psychotherapist first tried to help her get more in touch with what he considered the voice of reason within her. This reasonable self did not continually depreciate her. It made her feel worthwhile. It tried to help her structure her time so that she might begin to achieve some of her self-imposed goals. This reasonable self also gave her permission to relax and let go and experience the pleasure of the present, and it gave her guidance on how to practice interpersonal approach skills with people, both men and women.

The therapist saw that his task was to increase the frequency of statements from the reasonable self and to decrease or eliminate statements from the unreasonable self, her unrelenting and severe conscience. He first taught her meditation initiated by observing her respiration, as previously described herein. She was then told to watch her thoughts and was instructed that, whenever the unreasonable self was in predomination, she should disregard it and continue focusing on her breathing. Furthermore, she was instructed to observe her thoughts during the day, and whenever self-critical and self-punishing mental activities appeared, she was advised to let them flow away. To enhance the constructive effects of her reasonable self, he recommended that she could increase the probability of reasonable thoughts and feelings by making them occur before high-probability behavior. Since smoking was one of her high-probability behaviors, she was asked to put reasonable statements on small index cards and attach these to her cigarette carton. Before she smoked a cigarette (high-probability behavior), she was instructed to read and enjoy one of the note cards (low-probability feelings and behaviors). The statements that she compiled as emerging from her reasonable self were the following:

It's OK to do small things without feeling I'm a small person.

I am accepting myself more and more as I am, as I feel.

I am getting better-looking every day because the way I look is subjective.

I don't have to prove that I'm OK. I am OK because I exist.

Every day in every way I am getting better and better, more OK.

I don't have to become a star to accept myself or get acceptance from others.

Look, I don't have to set the world on fire. I can gradually listen to the inner voice. I can listen to the reasonable voice, not the one that's always putting me down.

More and more I seek, and believe that I am OK after all.

More and more I'm exposing myself as I am instead of what I'd like to be seen as.

On planning and structuring her time in the here-and-now to accomplish future goals, she listed:

I don't have to have instant gratification of each and every desire or impulse that arises.

More and more I am (in a relaxed way) thinking about planning what to do tomorrow—one day at a time.

I am learning more and more to distinguish reality from fantasy and wishful thinking.

I am taking one step at a time, and no step is too small.

More and more I am willing and able to recognize and manage my problems.

I don't have to immediately say anything or everything that comes into my mind.

I can increasingly be here now without escaping into fantasies, obstructions, illusions, nightmares.

More and more I am learning how to structure my own time.

Doing something is better than nothing at all: I am learning to quit the habit of not acting from fear of failing, and more and more I am looking for what I want to do and see.

On letting go, she listed:

Gradually I am opening myself to more pleasure and good feelings.

I am feeling more positive about myself, other people, and life every day.

I am easy with good feelings.

I am gradually increasing my tolerance of reasonable amounts of tension, uncertainty, ambiguity.

I am gradually becoming more and more flexible.

I will not constantly defer here-and-now enjoyment for that "big payoff."

I am more and more aware of the need to let go and am willing and able to let go, enjoy myself, and have fun.

On relaxing, she listed:

I will practice holding still, slowing down.

I am more and more aware of being willing and able to relax.

I am aware of breathing deeply and easily , and am
willing and able to do so.

On practicing social skills (increasing the probability of effective performance of overt behavior), she
listed:

More and more I am seeing people as they are,
without labels.
I am appreciating and enjoying and understanding
men as people more and more.
I am gradually increasing my eye contacts—with
practice.

During six months of largely self-treatment, with
occasional supervision from her psychotherapist, this
patient found a job for the first time in five years. She
began to date men, including one with whom she said
she had the most meaningful relationship she had ever
had with a man; this experience gave her hope that she
could learn to relate better to men.

6

Religious Approaches

Religious approaches to existential matters are designed to focus on both secular and everyday problems, and also on the broader problems involved with immortality. For many individuals, coming to a decision or reaffirming a belief system about immortality, about life after death, clears the way for improved coping with human life on this planet. Moreover, religious retreats, like vacations or holidays away from the regular routines of work, provide time for recreation and diversion, which in themselves prepare one to deal with the strains of loving and working. The uttering of familiar pledges of faith and the communal sharing of ritualistic activities and singing are all capable together of pro-

133

ducing peace of mind and the sense of being in the good graces of an all-powerful, all-knowing, and all-understanding deity. The mood created re-evokes the sense of being protected and being cared for that we all experienced in our infancy when we were helpless and were nurtured by loving caretakers. The re-experiencing of such a state and mood occurs also when we fall asleep. And this state, unquestionably, can recharge one's batteries, increase one's sense of purpose, and improve one's self-esteem. The reading of holy books and the reciting of prayers can also evoke such feelings and help sustain an individual through the stresses of everyday life and the need to cope with the more serious, inevitable hardships each one has to face.

EXAMPLES OF FAVORABLE RESULTS THROUGH SELF-PSYCHOTHERAPY MEDIATED BY RELIGIOUS MEANS

Testimonials of relief from existential anxieties have been reported by practically all adherents to most religious belief systems. In fact, the principal subject matter dealt with in most religions is aimed at providing comfortable answers to the questions we all uniformly raise about the goals of our existence and the mystery concerning life after death. This could also be said to be the purpose of most religions. Religious activities in which groups of people participate, sometimes augmented by the use of television, are recognized to have powerful effects on the sense of well-being and the relief of the sorrows common to mankind.

But what is the evidence that largely private sessions with oneself can facilitate such improvement of mental or physical disorders? Some religions foster retreats or a longer monastic life for their devotees; religiously infused literature is full of testimonials that such activities — characterized by the maintenance of silence, by self-scrutiny and concentrated reflection on one's moral character and the betterment of the relationship with one's God and/or the immutable laws of the universe — have tremendous healing qualities. This is one of the major reasons that religious approaches deserve to be included among the effective methods of self-healing and self-psychotherapy. In the third-world nations as well as in highly industrialized countries, large masses of individuals turn to and rely on religiously infused methods of providing answers to their existential questions, and, no less importantly, providing solace for the everyday problems and frustrations of living.

Is there not also some evidence in the medical or psychiatric literature of the potential influence of religious measures in alleviating illness? Pattison and his co-workers (1973) studied a group of forty-three fundamentalist–Pentecostal individuals who experienced seventy-one faith healings. Each individual was interviewed following a structured procedure to assess: (1) the person's life pattern prior to faith healing, (2) the person's life pattern following faith healing, (3) the person's medical history both before and after faith healing, and (4) how the individual perceived the function or purpose of faith healing. These researchers found that the faith healing, while it relieved the symptoms of the participants in the study, did not result in alternate symptom formation, nor did it eliminate other physical evidence of disease. The subject's symptoms were simply denied. Furthermore, a typical constellation of personality traits was found, including the use of denial of physical disability and emotional problems, repression (unconscious inhibition of feelings or thoughts), projection (attributing problems or difficulties to others rather than to oneself), and disregard of reality. These authors found that the primary function of faith healing was to reinforce a magical belief system, "ranging from witchcraft to Christian Science." This magical belief system was part of a coping method that was aimed at helping the individual adjust to problems associated with living, and at becoming better integrated in a religious subculture.

From this type of study, one must conclude that with respect to biological disorders that do indeed have a physiological basis, faith or religious healing effectively reduces or even eliminates the discomforts but has no favorable effect on the physical basis of the illness.

Another equally interesting study by Pattison and Pattison (1980) involved religiously mediated change in homosexuality. The authors evaluated eleven white men who claimed to have changed their sexual orientation from exclusive homosexuality to exclusive heterosexuality through religious participation. Although this change in sexual preference cannot be said to have come about solely through self-psychotherapy, for it was undoubtedly catalyzed by the religious ministrations of others, it can be surmised that considerable self-scrutiny and self-reflection were involved; detailed subjective reports on this process are not available. The authors reported that the average initial self-identification as a homosexual occurred at age 11 and that the average change to heterosexual identification occurred at age 23. The authors reported that eight of the men had become emotionally detached from their previous homosexual identity in both behavioral and intrapsychic processes. Three of the men were functionally heterosexual with some evidence of neurotic conflict over their sexuality. This study certainly suggests that rather pervasive personality changes can be brought about, at least in young individuals, through religious persuasion.

Perhaps the effectiveness of Alcoholics Anonymous in initiating and catalyzing personality changes should be mentioned here. Most professional psychotherapists have found that their work with certain alcoholics is unsuccessful unless the alcoholic can be persuaded to attend meetings of Alcoholics Anonymous. In addition to using the persuasive power of a group to bring about therapeutic effects on alcoholism, Alcoholics Anonymous promotes belief in a divine power—namely, a religious belief—to gain its therapeutic goals.

We should not overlook the fact that most military academies promote a belief in a deity, and have some kind of special reward system for those who hold such a belief. Hence, risking one's life in battle for one's country, with a special reward system in mind, becomes much easier for the soldier. That there are other methods besides a belief in a diety to motivate soldiers to fight hard, and expose themselves to a high possibility of getting killed, is certainly attested to by soldiers fighting for nations that espouse an atheistic or agnostic point of view.

EXAMPLES OF THE TREATMENT
OF GRIEF

Religiously Infused Methods

People who have strong convictions concerning the possibility of life after death or who devoutly believe that a deity will take care of them through eternity are able to bear the prospect of their own death and the death of dear ones with relative equanimity. These religious beliefs, reinforced through one's own mental reflections and self-assurances, appear to make martyrdom and dying for their country easier for many soldiers. The death of loved ones, for those who have a sense of certainty about a hereafter, can be experienced without going through the same painful and prolonged stages of grief and mourning suffered by nonbelievers. A pervasive religious belief forms a secure foundation for the self-psychotherapy involved in the process of loss and grief. John Wesley, Martin Luther, Abraham Lincoln, Albert Schweitzer, Florence Nightingale, Augustine, and the apostle Paul are all said to have been among the many people who were calm in the face of dying and death.

Nonreligious Methods of Coping with Grief

There are large numbers of people in this world who do not embrace a religion that provides them with equanimity about the matter of death. Are there successful methods of dealing with dying and death without the convincing belief that one is going on to another life or form of life beyond this world? Are there secular ways of making the passage easier? Modern wisdom on this issue favors allowing oneself to go through the grief process, instead of inhibiting it, by letting oneself cry openly over the impending or past loss of the loved one, as well as letting oneself ponder and reflect on the memories of experiences one had with this individual. Such reflection often tends to evoke more tears and grief, and encourages direct confrontation of one's terrible sense of loss. But the rationale for this approach to mourning is that it helps one make final farewells to the person who has passed away, and prevents delayed grief reactions which may be experienced months or years later in the form of disabling physical or mental illnesses. Although another person or persons may help to facilitate one's mourning, the brunt of the grief has to be privately experienced. And this kind of slow, persisting self-psychotherapy, colored by many different emotions — though sadness and associated feelings such as resentment and anxiety tend to predominate — is the nature of mourning for most of us. Normal grief can be differentiated from mental depression; normal grief involves the characteristics of mourning, but the mourner recovers in a shorter period of time than in the case of pathological depression. The mental and physiological symptoms of normal grief are more transient and not disabling.

Sometimes devout individuals are not able to cope well with the process of their own dying. Such a reaction is understandable. Let me illustrate by recounting the story of a religious man who was dying of cancer, but felt that God should spare him because he had led such a good life.

SELF-GRIEF AND INSUFFICIENT REWARD FOR RELIGIOUS FAITH

Faith

It was the fourth time in six months that Peter Smart had gone to the hospital for treatment of his spreading cancer. It had started in his prostate gland and spread to his back. Now there was some cancer in his right forearm. And it hurt.

He had started out in this situation feeling very confident that he would be cured. He was a good man who had turned many a person to Christ in the last twenty of his forty-six years. He had given up his vices, including the heavy boozing and the sinning with women. He had repented and done good works. In his heart and soul he knew he would be saved from this cancer because he had prayed and prayed. And he had asked of God, just this one time, to be allowed to be an exception. That was because he did not want to be called to Heaven now. He was not ready. He had important things he wanted to do yet.

At the first hospital he went to, he had an operation on his prostate gland. The doctor told him he had not been able to get out all of the tumor, because it had already spread. His doctor worked with other doctors, and they gave him some localized radiation treatment in the hope that that would clear it up. They also gave him some hormone treatment that they said would control it.

There's no point in going into any detail on how the operation felt. He had no fear before the operation, and he did not want to think or talk about how it felt afterward.

Right after he was released from that hospital, he

went to two faith-healing ceremonies, one in a big city auditorium and another in a huge tent. And he was cured. And he spoke the Word of Jesus to others, and they came and were healed.

Everything was fine for two months. Then he began to feel pain in his back, his lower back. So he went to see his doctor, who said there was a spread of his first cancer to his spine. He told this doctor he was wrong. He could not have a cancer spread because he had already had one operation, and also x-ray films there; and to make sure he was cured he had gone to faith healing twice, and to the best faith healers around. He forgave his doctor for blaspheming, but asked him to send him to another doctor. This time, he said, he wanted a doctor who was a believer.

The new doctor was a believer. He had Peter Smart go to another hospital that had a painting of Jesus on the Cross in the lobby. Some more radiation treatment was applied to his lower back, and he also got a chemical drug that would get rid of this new cancer. This drug made him lose his hair, but they said it would all grow back and not to worry.

However, he felt sort of sick in the stomach, and he lost his appetite. But he did not care. He knew his prayers were being answered, because he could sleep. And in his sleep he had a vision that he was being cured of his second cancer.

He was all right for three months. Then he got this bump on his right arm. It was hard, and it grew bigger. He did not want to go back to that second hospital again, but he did, and the doctor who was a believer told him it was a spread of his cancer.

Peter Smart just could not believe it. "My God, why hast thou forsaken me?" he asked. It could be just a test of his faith. But why would he — of all people on earth — be put to a test he did not need? He would never lose faith in his being healed. He was going to leave this doctor, though. He had heard of another doctor who was the best cancer specialist in the county. This doctor worked at the university. It did not matter whether this new doctor was a believer. He had him go to this great university hospital. So here he was.

The new doctor had lots of younger doctors around him, and all these doctors came into his hospital room and looked at him while the chief doctor talked to him and asked him questions. He looked at their faces while they were looking at him. And he could not figure out what they were thinking, because they had no expressions on their faces, except serious ones. The chief doctor had a nice friendly face.

After a week in this big university hospital, he had gone through all kinds of tests. Rodlike tubes were put up through his penis and his colon. Fancy x-ray pictures were taken of his spine, rectum, pelvis, chest, and even his head. A good deal of blood was drawn from the veins in his arms. Nobody — neither the doctors nor the nurses — talked much about what was going on or what they were finding out.

Then, after a week, the chief doctor dropped by with all his solemn-eyed younger doctors for a talk. The chief doctor said there had been some spreading of the cancer, yes. But they could slow it down by a little more radiation to his arm and to his back. And he promised that this would ease any pain. And the chief doctor said he was going to give him some medicine to also help ease the pain. And Peter Smart got some of that new medicine the very same day, which made him feel better even though he could read in the eyes of all those doctors that his condition was not good.

So when the doctors had been gone for a while, he got up out of his hospital bed and walked around the hospital floor. He walked through a door with a sign that read "Exit." It led to an outdoor balcony four flights up. He could look down below to the ground. This made him feel a bit dizzy. He tried putting one leg over the low outside wall. And he could just raise it high enough without unbearable pain to let it rest on the top of the wall. Just then a nurse came out and said to him, in a scolding fashion, "Mr. Smart, you're not supposed to be out here. Come in!" And she gently took his arm and led him back to his room. He did not mind very much because he felt extremely tired.

That day a different doctor came to see him with two younger doctors. This doctor said he was a psychiatrist and the other two doctors were too. And he said he was visiting Mr. Smart because he had heard Mr. Smart had worries and was behaving like he might seriously hurt himself. This doctor and the two younger doctors had friendly, not-so-solemn faces. The older doctor said they wanted to understand him, and to help him if he had any worries about himself or his condition. Somehow, this was just what Peter Smart wanted to hear. He poured out his heartfelt feelings to these people who listened without interrupting him. They had sympathetic faces. Mr. Smart told them about this cancer that he had and how he had asked God to spare him for a while, as he was not yet ready to leave this earth. He told them how he had done so many good works for God and for Jesus for so many years. He confided in them how he knew he could count on his prayers being answered. He showed the doctors all the cards and flowers he had from friends wishing him well. He dropped the name of a famous evangelist who had to come see him and to pray with him. He admitted, weeping a little and clumsily drying his eyes with a corner of his bedsheet, that he could not understand why he had to have this terrible thing at this time. It hurt his body and made him weak and tired. But, he said, he did not want to hurt himself more, for he was already hurting enough. He had just gone out onto the hospital balcony and looked down, and he had wondered for a moment what it would be like to crawl over the wall and drop down and quickly end his stay on the earth. He did not know how one of his legs got up on the wall. The medicine they had given him to ease his pain must have confused him, he offered. Why would he ever want to hurt himself permanently when he had faith that he would be taken care of by the Lord?

The listening doctors nodded affirmatively. And now Peter Smart asked them whether they believed he could be cured if he believed he would be? And the older psychiatrist said it often helped, and the two younger ones nodded assent. Thereupon, Peter Smart asked them to hold hands in a circle and pray with him, if they would, for help and peace. And the three doctors held hands with him and bowed their heads silently as he uttered a brief prayer.

Mr. Smart stayed in the hospital three more days. And on each day all his doctors, including the psychiatrists, came to see him.

A psychiatric consultation note was written on his medical chart, stating that he was depressed and potentially suicidal because of the grave prognosis of his metastatic carcinoma, and that he should be kept under close observation. He told his doctors that he would never lose faith. Finally he was sent home.

Three weeks after leaving the university hospital, Peter Smart passed away at home. Funeral services were held at his church. All his relatives and friends came to pay their last respects. He was buried at a pleasant cemetery, and a medium-sized stone marker was placed at the head of his grave.

7

Other Self-Psychotherapeutic Methods: Autogenic Training

In Germany in the 1930s, J. H. Schultz and W. Luthe developed "autogenic training," a medical treatment emphasizing self-control over autonomic nervous system functions. It is actually a series of orientations that a person imagines or suggests to himself or herself while in a comfortable and relaxed state. These orientations activate a visceral response, which deepens relaxation and is thought to increase the effectiveness of the body's self-healing properties.

To begin autogenic exercise, you lie comfortably on your back or on a recliner chair and repeat the phrase "I am at peace." Repeat it slowly, again and again, for about one minute. Make yourself concentrate on it. If you find your mind drifting, gently bring yourself back to it. After a minute of practice, you may rest and then repeat the same process again. Continue alternating between rest and concentration several more times. After you have practiced this initial phase, you are ready to add the six basic orientations. These are a series of commands or suggestions to your body to be practiced one at a time, each for a week or more. For good results, perform the exercise several times a day. You should be convinced that your body has accepted each orientation before going on to the next.

The six orientations are:

1. My right arm (for right-handed people) is very heavy.
2. My right hand is warm.
3. My pulse is calm and strong.
4. My breath is calm and regular.
5. My solar plexus is growing warm.
6. My forehead is pleasantly cool.

Begin with the first orientation. Suggest heaviness to your arm for a minute. Then alternate with a minute of rest, perhaps accompanied by the suggestion that you are at peace. Practice only this exercise for three to seven days. Then, one at a time, practice each succeeding orientation. In about two months you will be able to combine all the orientations and induce the whole set of changes in your body within minutes. The advocates of autogenic training claim that this kind of self-therapy is capable of reducing the tension and anxiety associated with many different conditions, and also of alleviating various psychosomatic disorders.

SELF-HYPNOSIS

Hypnosis is a state of increased suggestibility that can be induced by someone else or by oneself. Though this mental state should be distinguished from meditation it has some similarities to it, especially in the way it is brought about. Moreover, it has healing qualities for some people. How is self-hypnosis achieved?

First get yourself in a comfortable position. You have to either sit or lie down. Now focus your eyes intently on a small area directly ahead of you until your eyes feel tired and your vision begins to become blurred. Roll your eyeballs upward and close your eyelids. Imagine that you feel a warm cloud over the center of your body, and as the cloud touches you, let it warm and relax that part of your body. Next, imagine that the cloud is expanding from the center of your body and growing larger and touching each part of your body in turn with its calming warmth. Let yourself become totally bathed in the energizing cloud while it releases any tensions within you.

While you are completely engulfed in the cloud, let your body become lighter, warmer, and relaxed. Let yourself imagine that you are weightless and can float upward and soar into the sky. While you remain at the center of this cloud, let it take you to a special place where you can be entirely relaxed, calm, and at peace. See how beautiful that place is and how it looks, smells, sounds, and tastes. Realize how pleasant you feel in that cloud and how relaxed, warm, healthy, protected, and sheltered you feel. You can enjoy the pleasure of complete well-being.

When you decide to leave this ideal state, simply

imagining yourself going up again in the cloud and then being gently settled back into your room. Before opening your eyes and completing your return, however, let yourself spend a moment recalling how you have felt. Remind yourself that you can re-experience that ideal state any time you desire. Take along with you that feeling of peace and well-being for the remainder of the day. When you feel prepared, open your eyes and sit quietly for a few minutes.

Some individuals use this technique to achieve a state of mental relaxation before going to work or to sleep. Using this approach provides a feeling, for some individuals, that they can exercise a measure of control over a hectic and disturbing life, enabling them to gain some sense of relief and tranquility.

HYPNOSIS AND SELF-HYPNOSIS IN TERMINAL CANCER

Sam was a 35-year-old married physician who developed an adenocarcinoma of the rectum. The cancer was very malignant and even after an extensive surgical procedure to remove all evidence of it, the cancer spread throughout his body. Sam was openly enraged at having this incurable disease. He was a handsome, happily married man with two children; he was successfully engaged in his medical practice, and his general physical condition was excellent. During the terminal stages of his cancer, although his wife, family, and many friends spent much time with him, he suffered considerable pain. His physician gave him whatever pain-relieving medication he requested. In spite of this, he continued to complain of pain.

He requested that a psychiatrist, who was a close friend of his, hypnotize him and give him post-hypnotic suggestions so that he would no longer suffer pain. His psychiatrist told him that there was a serious question whether hypnosis could relieve his pain if the analgesic medication he was receiving did not do so. After all, the psychiatrist said, hypnosis was only a heightened state of suggestion. Sam said he already knew this, but he still wanted to give hypnosis a try. Accordingly, the psychiatrist hypnotized Sam and in addition to telling him that he would be relieved of all pain for twenty-four hours after the hypnotic state was ended, he told Sam that he would be able through self-hypnosis to bring on the hypnotic state himself and relieve his pain whenever it returned. Much to everyone's surprise, Sam had immediate pain relief after his hypnotic state was ended. And for almost two days he felt no pain, for he used the self-hypnosis that his psychiatrist had recommended. Then his pain symptoms began to recur and the psychiatrist returned to re-hypnotize Sam and suggest post-hypnotic pain relief as he had done previously. The pain relief was immediate and this time it lasted for ninety-six hours. Throughout the remainder of Sam's life, brief hypnosis and self-hypnosis made the quality of his existence tolerable.

SELF-PSYCHOTHERAPY WITH CRYSTALS

A type of self-psychotherapy that attributes powerful healing qualities to crystals has recently become popular. As with religions, the devotees of this method project the source of the therapeutic force externally. In this case the source is crystals, rather than a deity or Nature. In two short volumes, Dolfyn (1987) details this approach.

The rationale is appealingly simple, as explained in the lead paragraph in volume 1. Crystals, according to Dolfyn, express the unity of the four elements: earth, fire, water, and air. They grow in the earth and remind us of the mineral evolution of this planet. They can transmit a piezoelectric charge, and hence they are also expressions of fire. They have water in their molecular structure, and they have an icelike appearance. And crystals, like air, let light pass through them. Therefore, in Dolfyn's view, when you carry a crystal you are carrying all the elements of creation.

A beginner is advised to select a crystal having only one point. When trying out various crystals, holding them one by one in your hand, the crystal you feel drawn to is the one you should buy. The way to tune to it, according to Dolfyn, is to live with the crystal for a while, sleep with it under your pillow and hold it in your hand while awake. Meditate with it, peer at the moon and stars through it, look at your nearby sur- roundings through it, speak to it, and even say your prayers through it. Getting tuned to the crystal involves thinking of the crystal as alive. Such thinking is called "animistic"—that is, thinking that considers an object as animate, in contrast to inanimate; "anthropomor- phic" thinking, on the other hand, ascribes human qualities to the object. Teachers of crystal therapy tell you to let the crystal rest among potted plants. You are advised to place it in the sun or the rain, or in a stream, lake, or ocean. A state of not discriminating between something alive and not alive is fostered by your being told to introduce your crystal to your favorite places and your favorite seasons of the year. This keeps you tuned to your crystal so that the magical intuitive child in you is awakened. This is said to be the part of your being that best communicates with a crystal. This process prepares you for being highly suggestible and not differentiating yourself with respect to person, place, and time.

This state allows what Sigmund Freud referred to as "primary process thinking," the state predominating in the id, an unconscious primitive portion of the self in which the sexual and aggressive instincts reign. Here no distinctions are made between persons, places, or times. Magical wish-fulfillment can be initiated by your self and transferred to a benign, loving, all-powerful, godlike object that you can hold in your hand.

This is a kind of self-psychotherapy. The favorable effects achieved, if any, are reflections of your own hopeful and optimistic views of yourself and the world, and your capacity to have a belief and conviction that the forces influencing the course of life are more good than evil. In simpler terms, this reflects the power of positive thinking. You should note here that crystal therapy has similarities to self-hypnosis; the difference is that self-hypnosis dispenses with the crystal. Crystal therapy is similar to hypnosis using an external hypnotist (the crystal) which you have programmed.

Devotees of crystal therapy recognize that other self-psychotherapies can prepare you for favorable influences via crystals, for they advise combining meditation with crystal healing. The reader will also note that behavior and conditioning self-psychotherapy has some similarities to crystal healing. In both methods, positive statements about one's abilities to reach specified goals (for example, "I am getting better and better in every way" or "I am becoming more beautiful, for beauty is subjective") are rehearsed mentally in order to reinforce and shape your behavior and thoughts. Behavior and conditioning self-psychotherapy, however, does not attribute magical qualities to crystals; it relies on scientifically based experimental and natural-history studies that demonstrate that conditioned responses (classical and operant) can be potentiated through appropriate and timely positive reinforcement.

There is no scientific evidence to support the hypothesis that crystals respond to the immediate human and nonhuman environment in the ways that the teachers of crystal healing claim. Nor is there any empirical evidence that crystals do exert healing influences or have telepathic ability or power. The healing effects are illusory and not unlike those described by Pattison and colleagues (1973) in the faith healing activities of the Pentecostal and Christian Science religions. On the other hand, if you should inquire whether symptoms and distress can be relieved through belief systems that have no scientific basis, the answer would have to be in the affirmative. Elsewhere in this book I indicate that part of the basis of the psychogenic cure is a belief that the method one is using will work. Religious beliefs, belief in the magical power of crystals, and belief in the power of someone's will (including one's own) to reach a goal, as in hypnosis and self-hypnosis, can sometimes relieve some subjective symptoms such as anxiety and depression and even pain. (See the example of pain relief through hypnosis in the case of Sam p. 152) And physicians can tell you that some patients do get relief from their symptoms when given a placebo, a form of medication that contains no more than inert ingredients. But these procedures have not succeeded in curing those diseases modern medicine classifies as incurable (as in the case of "Faith," p. 140). The symptomatic relief available through these methods should not, however, be overlooked. Relief of existential anxiety and depression through religious and nonreligious intervention is far from a trivial matter, as in both of these case histories. And evidence of favorable psychosomatic effects of these and other self-psychotherapy methods on the course of some physical and mental disorders, also documented here, is worthy of attention.

8

The Middle Period

of Self-Analysis and

Self-Psychotherapy

Self-psychotherapy will proceed following the technique typical for each different kind of psychotherapy, whether it be psychoanalysis or any variant of it, behavior therapy, meditation, self-hypnosis, one of the religious processes, and so forth. The progress made and the duration of time involved will depend, of course, on the goals set and whether they involve only a minor aspect of your life or your personality, or a major one. With all these self-help processes, as with learning processes involving a professional external psychotherapist, there are obstacles and pitfalls which need to be appreciated and understood. Let us consider some of these.

COPING WITH SOME DETERRENTS

Decreasing Motivation

The subjective feelings most individuals begin to experience after making some initial progress is simply a gradual loss of interest in whatever self-psychotherapy one was using. There could be a number of reasons for such a feeling. Hopefully, the best reason might be that whatever approach you were using was successful in achieving your aims. Quite often such circumstances constitute the main reason for losing interest.

A more insidious reason could be that self-psychotherapy requires perseverance and patience, and the results, though they may be encouraging, do not come fast enough. Relatively trivial goals are easier to reach, whereas more ambitious goals involving deeper personality changes are more difficult. Moreover, some people have what might be called "low frustration tolerance"; that is, they give up easily. This trait can prevent a person's making much progress in any endeavor. Such a trait can become a typical and habitual feature of a person, even reaching neurotic proportions. If so, it is a problem that deserves to be focused upon through some form of self-psychotherapy. If an individual really wants to try to overcome a low frustration tolerance, it can be done. Many different reasons may lie behind this trait, such as the viewpoint that success should come to you easily regardless of how difficult it is for others to achieve; or such long-standing low self-esteem that the individual is defeated in his or her goals almost before setting out. To get at the underlying characteristics of such a low frustration tolerance, a self-psychoanalytic approach is recommended with the main goal being to determine what these characteristics are and how to decrease their effect. However, whatever kind of self-psychotherapy one uses to change this paralyzing trait, steps have to be taken to break or alter it. And those steps involve forcing oneself to persevere and keep on practicing the psychotherapeutic approach no matter how fatigued or discouraged one gets. For a person with low frustration tolerance, there are advantages in practicing the completion of various tasks that one was not good at staying with previously. The more such a person can continue working at various problems that would previously have been abandoned too early, in frustration over delayed success, the more self-confidence can be built up. And the more the possibility that such successes can be generalized and contribute to the individual's progress in different forms of psychotherapy.

Distractions

Most types of self-psychotherapy require large amounts of time and attention directed to oneself. The interruptions of television or radio, and social or domestic distractions, can interfere with setting aside effective time for one's self-psychotherapy. A time must be chosen when there is a good possibility that one will not be interrupted and can enjoy relative quiet. For many individuals, establishing a regular time to practice self-psychotherapy pays good dividends in that the goals one sets for oneself are more likely to be reached.

Preference for Alcohol
and Other Chemical Substances

Most of us are sometimes tempted to seek quick and easy solutions to life's problems. Alcohol, marijuana, PCP, cocaine, heroin, and other drugs of this type can relieve emotional pain or distress and provide some temporary distraction. The adverse effects of these different chemical substances have become well known; many books have been written about alcohol and drug abuse. These substances when abused never solve problems. Rather, they create problems, often new ones that cannot be remedied.

There are many new kinds of psychoactive drugs that have psychotherapeutic effects. These include the so-called major tranquilizers, the antidepressants, the minor tranquilizers, the psychomotor stimulants, the anticonvulsants, the analgesics (pain-killers), and so on. Under a physician's care, these medicaments can be very helpful and useful for the right patient, at the right time, under some circumstances. They may, for example, relieve certain symptoms, such as anxiety, more rapidly than any form of psychotherapy. They are not designed, however, to provide insight regarding the causes of one's anxiety. Nor can they provide a sense of mastery over one's emotions. They are not necessarily antagonistic to or in competition with the psychotherapeutic approaches, but rather can be used — under special circumstances in which they appear to be medically required — together with the psychotherapy, whether the latter is being carried out by oneself or under the guidance of a therapist. A fuller discussion of the pros and cons of psychotherapy versus pharmacotherapy is beyond the scope of this book.

Privacy and Confidentiality

Most psychotherapeutic procedures involving a therapist, whether a professional clinician or a member of the clergy, evoke feelings of shame over the exposure of personal or private thoughts, feelings, and behaviors. Empathic and skillful therapists understand and appreciate this reaction and try to decrease and allay it. What helps most patients in the process of revealing information about themselves is the assurance that the information will be held confidential. Even with this reassurance, patients often spend considerable time covering up their private memories and experiences, or suffering shame and embarrassment during the process of exposing them. Much reassurance is likely to be required during psychotherapy to help such people realize that the therapist does not ostracize or repudiate his or her patients.

With self-psychotherapy, there is an initial advantage of keeping the inner details of the process and the personal discoveries private and confidential. Leaving personal notes and journals around that others might inadvertently read is not a good idea. Discoveries by others of private matters revealed in the middle of a personal psychotherapy might inhibit such work. This does not mean that you should not, after your own self-psychotherapy has achieved its initial aims, share your discoveries and personal achievement with significant others. The point here is that premature sharing with others about such matters, before you have completed acquiring a good understanding of yourself, may lead you to reveal details about yourself that you will change your mind about after you have finished a complete chapter of your personal psychotherapy. Also, if you put yourself into a position where you think you have to tell someone each detail of self-discovery as it unfolds, this very fact may inhibit your wanting to uncover new details because you fear you will have to reveal some secrets you are not ready to share.

Wish to Change the Goals of Self-Psychotherapy

After a trial of psychotherapy everyone finds it useful to examine his or her original goals and to determine whether these have been reached. Unfortunately, when obtaining psychotherapy with some therapists the goals are not always carefully spelled out, or are lost sight of during the therapeutic process. This problem needs to be avoided in any form of self-psychotherapy. The goals should be formulated from the beginning, and periodically reviewed to establish to what extent they have been realized. If they have not been fully reached, then one should continue trying to do so or maybe consider changing them. Or, if you are satisfied with what you have accomplished, you may want to pursue a different goal. Now is the time to decide which of the different kinds of psychotherapy would be most suitable for the purpose of obtaining the new goals. That is, one of the types of psychotherapy you have not been using may be better under these new circumstances than the one you have been using.

Wish to Change the Method of Self-Psychotherapy

As I have just pointed out, some kinds of psychotherapy are better suited to reach certain goals than others. And some therapists have more aptitude in the use of one type of psychotherapy than in another. So feel free to experiment and learn which kind of therapeutic technique comes easily to you and at the same time gets the results you want. Some kinds of psychotherapy, such as psychoanalysis, are rather complicated and require practice and patience and a fair amount of intellectual interest and skill. Other types, like meditation, may be relatively easy to master, at least for some people. But remember that each of these different psychotherapies facilitates working toward some goals but not others. Take a look again at the section of this book that discusses the goals of therapy and selecting which method to use. Then make a new selection.

RECOGNIZING PROGRESS

Using the Self-Psychoanalytic Method

The psychoanalytic method should provide insight and understanding about the psychosocial origins and development of your emotional problems, including some perspectives you did not have previously. It should give you some ideas on why and how you have dealt with various troublesome life situations. It should help you distinguish between the types of people and life contexts you experienced in the past, and those of the present. It should encourage you to alter your internalized viewpoints about people, places, and situations so that your emotional and intellectual concepts of these are less extreme, and more flexible, tolerant, and accepting. It should help you rediscover memories of your early childhood that may throw light on why you feel and behave as you do in the present. Your self-esteem should improve and your general level of anxiety and depression decrease. Your equanimity should become better, and you may find that you now have the option of exploring new methods of coping and dealing with daily problems.

Using Self-Psychotherapy for Existential Goals

Several different types of psychotherapy are capable of tackling existential problems—that is, problems involving questions or issues about the purposes of existence. In brief, what is life all about? What are we supposed to do on this planet? What happens to us after we die?

You should get some answers to these kinds of questions through one of the forms of self-psychotherapy. Faith in a religious belief may come to provide some guidelines on how to conduct your behavior throughout your existence. On the other hand, you may decide that an organized religious system is not so attractive to you, or you may feel drawn to believe in one that is different from the one in which you were raised. Or, usually more difficult, you may decide to live out your life in the best way you can and not to worry very much about what is going to happen to you after you pass away.

Quite often, existential issues come back periodically throughout one's lifespan asking for a reconsideration and a reaffirmation or refutation. If one episode of self-psychotherapy has come up with satisfying answers for the moment, do not be surprised if some of the same old issues or some new ones surface and require reconsideration in the future.

Using the Meditative Approach

The enthusiasts of meditation claim that meditation can relieve anxiety and depression, provide answers to existential questions, relieve various psychosomatic ailments such as migraine headaches, and even stop the spread of cancer. There is supportive evidence that bad moods and some somatic complaints — that is, physical symptoms — can be eased in some people, using meditative approaches. Convincing scientific evidence that meditation can change the course of malignant forms of cancer has not been forthcoming. The most advanced medical forms of cancer treatment, such as surgery and chemotherapy, have steadily made valid inroads against formerly incurable forms of cancer. That any kind of psychotherapy, including meditative, visual-imaging, or psychoanalytic approaches, are capable in themselves of preventing or curing malignant forms of cancer, has yet to be proven. However, no one is likely to take the viewpoint that having a hopeful attitude, and maintaining a high quality of life, is unwise or has an adverse effect on the course of cancer or any other physical disorder; and if these viewpoints can be achieved through the use of any of the psychotherapies, then they should be used for such purposes.

Using Other Psychotherapeutic Approaches

There are many other types of psychotherapies. In some instances, they have acquired identifying titles or names. In other instances, a professional psychotherapist has written about a type of psychotherapy without attributing a special name to it. In order to recognize whether any progress has been achieved by using the psychotherapy, all that is necessary is to review systematically what one originally wanted to achieve, and then evaluate whether or not these goals have been reached.

In the case of psychotherapies which have been named and studied, as in the following examples, it is easy to evaluate the results to determine how much headway has been achieved.

The "Trial-Run" Approach

Here one hopes to achieve therapeutic results by trying out a new approach or solution to a behavioral or emotional problem. The different adaptive or coping method, like a change in a tennis or golf stroke, needs practice to perfect and a period of time to determine whether it achieves better results than the previous method.

The "Reality Therapy" Approach

The focus of "reality therapy" is upon making one better able to face the real world, to avoid or discard irrational or inappropriate perceptions of others or oneself, and to develop the use of effective coping methods to deal with today's problems. Many different kinds of psychotherapies employ this kind of focus at some stage in the therapy. A review of how realistic are one's perceptions of the outside world and oneself, and how realistic are one's coping methods, is applicable to most therapies and problems.

The "Abreactive" Approach

"Abreaction" refers to the bringing out of a suppressed complex or a desire either by acting it out or by talking it out. For example, you might work through or resolve grief over a loved one's illness or death by talking about every detail of the experiences you had together. This may evoke tears and feelings of sadness. This process is one way you can help yourself to effectively make your farewells and give up the attachment. Not letting yourself experience the pain of grief can make it difficult or impossible to form new attachments and to go on with the business of living.

So if you have been caught up in an unresolved grief reaction involving some kind of past loss, whether the loss involves a person, place, thing, or job, it is a good idea to try to evaluate whether you have made any significant progress in going through the grief process — whether you have done the necessary crying inside and outside over what has been lost. It is a sign of progress if you can say to yourself — and can believe — that whatever happened is "water under the bridge," or that one must "live and learn" or "win one and lose one." Commitment to new attachments or exploring new ways of doing things can be difficult if the abreactive approach is not used to some extent in dealing with such problems.

In self-psychotherapy, since there is no other person to talk to except oneself, you have to reflect — usually but not necessarily in silence — about all the events and experiences you ever had with the person, place, thing, or situation. Such reflection should continue until you have an emotional reaction, whether it is sadness and tears or resentment and clenched fists. And this kind of experience may have to be gone through many times privately before noticeable results can be recognized.

The "Confessional" Approach

In many different kinds of psychotherapy, sharing with another human being the shame or guilt you have been suffering from may help to account for the sense of relief, and the decrease in the plaguing depression, that result from the therapy. Some religions and certain group organizations like Alcoholics Anonymous make good use of the curative aspects of confession. Obviously, in self-psychotherapy one has to find a way to excuse oneself from oppressive shame or guilt. If the shame or guilt is real — that is, if one really did steal money from someone or cause a fatal injury, it may be difficult to decrease such feelings unless one can make some type of restitution or otherwise make up for the error. Atonement or penance does work, and certain actions toward remedying this real sense of error do help. When there is no way one can provide restitution, some type of penance may be beneficial. There are individuals who have no sense of shame or guilt over real events involving the exploitation of others; however, it is unlikely that very many such individuals would bother to read a book like this or care to deal with such matters of conscience.

Irrational shame and/or guilt are the stuff that psychoneuroses are made of. The various psychotherapies described herein are designed to deal in various ways — some more effectively than others — with irrational or excessive shame and/or guilt. Self-scrutiny and self-reflection can help you recognize whether you have made any decisive headway in relieving these feelings.

An Example of Successful Self-Psychotherapy Facilitated through Writing a Journal

A 25-year-old woman, employed as a marketing agent for a newspaper chain, sought psychotherapeutic help for episodic anxiety accompanied by concomitant involuntary nervous system symptoms, such as palpitations and "butterflies in her stomach," which occurred especially in situations at work. These symptoms appeared when her boss seemed overly critical of her, or appeared distant, or when she had to travel to cities like Chicago or New York, representing her company, and men made advances toward her. An extraordinarily attractive woman, she explained that she was happily married and wanted to observe her bond of loyalty to her husband, and yet she was conscious of feeling lonesome for companionship on these trips. Her anxiety symptoms, along with the accompanying physiological disturbances, seriously interfered with the efficiency she expected of her performance at work. In exploring her past family and social history, her psychotherapist discovered an experience she had had as a result of stressful circumstances, and this discovery can be seen to illustrate the successful use of self-psychotherapy in a person who has had no previous experience in this sort of process.

The patient grew up in a part of the United States that she has always considered close to a paradise — namely, Newport Beach, California, where the weather is perfect because it is never too warm or too cold, and the beautiful Pacific Ocean is nearby. More importantly, she was the second child of what she had considered a blissfully happy marriage; her parents never argued or disagreed with one another in front of the children, her father provided a superior standard of living, and insofar as she knew, her parents were deeply in love with one another. One day during her sixteenth year, a day which she could never forget, her father announced to the family that he no longer loved her mother, that he was divorcing her, and that he was moving away from their home to live by himself. She was so shocked by this surprising announcement and by her father's departure that she felt her whole world was coming to a sudden end. She felt that there was no way that she could sustain her grief and there was no one to turn to for solace. Her father was unrelenting in his determination to terminate the marriage, her mother was not available for sympathy and was trying to cope with her own distress by an excessive use of alcohol, which had previously been the case as well, and her older sister was herself overwhelmed. And although the father recognized the usefulness of professional counseling under such circumstances, the patient learned that marital counseling for her parents had been tried without avail, and that neither parent considered professional psychotherapy for their children might be timely and appropriate.

Somewhere, the patient had read that keeping a diary or journal had helped people overcome the wrenching pain of intolerable life situations. So she began to keep a journal, and she wrote in it regularly from the age of 16 to 18. She told her journal everything she felt and thought, following an approach of free association. She even recorded her dreams, many of which had a nightmarish quality during the first few months after she had learned of her parents' forthcoming divorce.

Now at the age of 25, she related to her psychotherapist that immediately after her father's crushing announcement, she had become conscious of suicidal ideas and wishes. She wrote about these in her diary. And eventually she got around to expressing her resentment toward her parents for always keeping their disagreements secret and for customarily portraying a completely agreeable couple in front of their children. Later she told her diary of her anger toward both parents for disrupting the security of their home, and expressed her suspicion that they did not love her and her sister enough to keep their marriage intact. She wrote that she wondered whether there might be some disappointment in her behavior, by one or both of her parents, that could have played a part in the events leading to the divorce.

After keeping her journal faithfully for two years, she realized that she had overcome the psychological blow she had suffered on learning of the end of her family life. She recalled that she had suffered not only a depressed mood but a recurring anxiety over her sense of the instability of human relations, especially if she could not even count on her own parents. This was often accompanied by an upset stomach and heart palpitations. When she stopped writing in her diary, she still felt sad about what had happened to her parents' marriage and their home, but she no longer felt suicidal or anxious about the stability of the relationships between herself and others. At this time in her life, she had gone on to college and was making good grades. She was certainly popular with young men, and had good relations with other women.

When she was 25, her psychotherapist asked her to bring in the journal she had written between the ages of 16 and 18. She did so, and it confirmed what she had related to him. He recognized that this was an excellent example of the effectiveness, even the life-saving potential, of self-psychotherapy, and he resolved to communicate this story someday at the right time and the right place. And that is why and how I can relate this true story here, for I was that psychotherapist.

A postscript might be appropriate here. The psychic trauma to the emotional security of her world at 16 made this patient vulnerable in later life to situations in which she might be made to feel unloved, or fearful that the outcome of some life situation might be in jeopardy. When she came to realize the connection between that teen-age experience with her family and her later experiences at work when she reached 25, all of her psychological and physiological symptoms gradually disappeared.

9

Terminal Phases

of Self-Analysis

and Self-Psychotherapy

In the preceding section, we have looked at how to recognize whether progress is being made during the course of different kinds of self-psychotherapy. Now we will examine how to determine whether a point has been reached at which it can be terminated.

Similar considerations need to be addressed whether one is working alone or with a professionally trained therapist of any calling. Have the initial goals been reached? Have the main problems which led one to seek psychotherapy been resolved? Is there other unfinished work to do? If progress has been made toward remedying problems or shortcomings, has the degree of personal change that is desired been achieved? In the course of one's therapy have new perspectives been awakened regarding additional goals that had not previously been realized? A good professional therapist constantly reviews these issues and reminds his patient that they should be evaluated thoroughly before termination of the therapy takes place. Obviously, in the process of any kind of self-psychotherapy, the patient is obliged to play also the role of his or her own therapist and needs to ask these same questions of him- or herself.

In such a process of self-examination, easy and modest goals are likely to have been met. And ambitious and complex goals may still be out of reach. Goals that require major personality changes are difficult to come by, even with an expert psychotherapist, and may take years to reach. So one cannot expect to reshape one's habitual ways of doing things or feeling about important matters any faster or more efficiently by any type of self-psychotherapy, as compared with using a professional therapist. While we are making such a comparison, it must be acknowledged at this point that not all professional therapists are equally adept or successful at solving the mental problems of other people. But the same statement can be made about being one's own psychotherapist — there is a broad range of individual differences and skills in the effectiveness with which people are capable of successful and productive self-scrutiny, self-discovery, and self-change.

ANALYZING THE DEGREE OF SUCCESS IN MAKING PROGRESS

One should use the following guidelines in analyzing the degree of self-psychoanalytic success that has been accomplished.

1. Review your initial goals and the extent to which they have been reached.

2. Review any possible changes made in the initial goals and the extent to which these may have been realized.

3. If some of the goals have not been reached, try to evaluate whether the unreached goals were unrealistic or whether they simply require more therapy—or whether they require the passage of time alone, as might be the case in the process of grieving for a lost person, place, or time in one's life.

4. Some goals may be of such a nature that they require endless self-examination and self-modification, such as the goal of keeping in continual touch with one's marginal or unconscious feelings or perfecting one's skills at a recreational sport or at a vocation. Such goals require a lifetime of self-observation and therapy and do not have a predetermined termination date for the process of self-psychotherapy.

5. Some goals cannot be achieved using the form of self-psychotherapy one selected, but may possibly be achieved using a different form. Hence, a different approach might be considered. Sometimes, in such instances, professional consultation with an expert might be sought. Many professionals might be wary of the success achievable through some form of self-psychotherapy, and thus automatically favor the use of a professionally trained therapist. This should be understandable, for presumably the professional spent many years studying under the tutelage of such experts in this field and has acquired creditable skills. So in obtaining a professional opinion regarding oneself, one should first look into how flexible this professional is

regarding self-help psychotherapy, in order to be sure there is no bias.

FURTHER OBSERVATIONS CONCERNING READINESS FOR TERMINATION

What Events or Factors Contributed to the Problems?

During the process of evaluation you must deal with the issue of whether or not you are ready to terminate your self-psychotherapy. You want to be certain that you have systematically reached a decision concerning which events and/or factors caused the problems that led you to seek psychotherapy.

Self

Was there some abnormality or unusual characteristic of your self that made you vulnerable to the problem, such as a low self-esteem, a very suspicious view of others or the world, an irrational fear or many fears, a sad or depressed state of mind, or considerable bottled-up anger? You want to be sure you have come to understand how these attitudes or feelings originated and why they may have persisted. You would like to be assured that these have diminished to the point where you are able to be more comfortable. You would like to know that self-psychotherapy has enabled you to find better ways of coping with these matters.

Others

The behavior or actions of others may have been the primary factor influencing your emotions and behavior. If so, did you discover some way or ways to deal with such an interpersonal matter? The precise interpersonal problem, and the method or methods of self-psychotherapy that you have chosen, will affect what you do about this. The loss of a loved one requires going through the painful process of grieving, and this takes time. A marital conflict or lover's conflict can be helped by self-psychotherapy that enables you to come to terms with what you must do about the situation. It might lead you to a decision to try couple's therapy or to require the other person to seek psychotherapeutic help. You may decide to enlarge your own social sphere — that is, to widen or improve your own social activities. There are too many possibilities to try to consider all of them here.

A Current Stressful Life Situation

Your problem might be primarily the result of a stressful life situation. For example, an auto accident you were in could have made you fearful of driving, anxious about other life situations, and troubled with nightmares. Or you might be employed in a troublesome location or occupation. Or you could have been discharged from your job. Life circumstances can be unpredictable and cruel. Self-psychotherapy may have to be designed to help one "roll with the punches," to adjust to and cope with the hardships.

Stressful Past Experiences

A contributing factor to your current life problem may be the recurring and haunting effects of life events that occurred some time ago. You will want to have developed some insight into what the immediate effects of those past experiences were, and whether their effects on your personality have changed over the months or years. The ideal way in which we aspire to deal with life's tragedies and sorrows is to try to be dignified, brave, and persevering, and to keep plodding onward. Such exemplary behavior is not always so easy. Self-psychotherapy may be useful in providing some effective ideas on how to accept and cope with the continuing stress of difficult past events.

Painful Memories

Current or past stressful experiences may lead to painful memories as one of the obsessive aftermaths of these events. You want to see whether self-psychotherapy has eased the pain of these memories, or has helped you find ways to "change the channel" and turn them off instead of allowing them to intrude on your mind when you were not choosing to think about them.

Temporary or Passing Events

A contributing factor may be a stressful person, place, or thing that will be gone in the near future. The various psychotherapies that have been discussed can often relieve the tension and distress brought on by these transient events.

Searching for and Using
the Best Coping Mechanisms

Consider whether you have found some better ways to deal with your problem. Symptoms of anxiety, depression, anger, and irritability are all signs that the methods we are using to deal with our problems, though they may be the best ones we could find by ourselves, are not the only ones and certainly not the best ones. The self-psychotherapies described in this book should be able to help us find better coping strategies.

Giving Oneself Time

In addition to the curative and healing aspects of the psychotherapies, another important factor has to be considered. That factor is the passage of time. Incorporating new ideas and new ways of thinking, feeling, and behaving requires patience and time enough for these new patterns to become part of oneself. Several months should elapse after one has stopped any kind of psychotherapy to decide how effective and successful it has been.

Afterword

RECURRENCES OF SYMPTOMS AND SIGNS OF ONE'S OLD PROBLEMS

It is not unusual for some of the symptoms and signs of your old problems to return. If and when they do, try to determine the triggers. Consider the possible contributing events and factors that have been discussed. Can any of the effects of these be minimized or avoided? If so, try to do that.

If you have found one or another kind of self-psychotherapy helpful, try it again. Usually, if such therapy has been previously useful, it will be so again.

CONCLUDING OBSERVATIONS

This self-help book was not written without conflict. Its major aim is to help individuals understand themselves and others, and to promote well-being through the improvement of their emotional and behavioral problems. It does not try to deal thoroughly with every kind of problem that one might encounter in life, nor does it seek to describe exhaustively every kind of therapy that might be applicable. Rather, it focuses on a limited group of self-help psychotherapies with more concentration on psychoanalytically oriented therapies than on other approaches. Such a selection is not, however, the major source of conflict, for an encyclopedic textbook was never the intention of this project. The major source of conflict is how to promote self-psychotherapy while maintaining the high standards set by science (rather than by nonscientific belief systems) and by professional organizations involved in training and certifying psychotherapists, such as the American Psychiatric Association, the American Psychoanalytic Association, and the American Psychological Association. Can a person who is not professionally trained, except for having read a book on the subject, actually and successfully gain symptomatic relief from—and intellectual insight into—his or her own emotional and behavioral problems? If the author did not believe this question could be answered affirmatively, writing this book would never have been attempted. But not everyone has the psychological-mindedness and intuitive skills to be able to benefit from such a book. With assistance from a professionally trained therapist, probably a larger percentage of individuals could benefit from such bibliotherapy. Systematic studies should be carried out to determine the extent to which this general issue can be answered affirmatively. Such studies could also determine to what extent each of the various methods described herein can remedy the problems of readers when practiced as self-psychotherapy, even when there is sound scientific evidence supporting the effectiveness of the method as it is used by professionally trained and certified therapists. This is the heart of the conflict involved in writing this book. The conflict can be largely resolved by advising the reader that some educational research needs to be done to substantiate to what extent and how well the ideas recommended in this book can work for every reader.

The aims and conflicts experienced by the author have been voiced by other professional workers in the field. Miller (1979) has encouraged psychotherapists to learn how to help people help themselves. Robitscher (1980) has warned against commercializing psychiatric knowledge. And Rosen (1987) has recently discussed self-help treatment books and their value, but has pointed out the limitations of their usefulness on grounds similar to those expressed by this author.

Freud (1957) was initially an enthusiast of self-analysis. He wrote, "I soon saw the necessity of carrying out a self-analysis, and this I did with a series of my own dreams which led me back through all the events of childhood: and I am still of the opinion today that this kind of analysis may suffice for anyone who is a good dreamer and not too abnormal" (p. 20). Later, he took a less favorable view of his self-analysis, writing, "I can only analyze myself with the help of knowledge obtained objectively (as from an outsider)" (p. 21). He also said, "In self-analysis the danger of incompleteness is particularly great. One is too soon satisfied with a part explanation, behind which resistance may easily be keeping back something that is more important perhaps."

With all these reservations in mind about the degree of success possible from using the self-help psychotherapies described here, it is fair to state that there is no risk involved in trying out these methods on oneself. For some readers the results will be very gratifying. And for some, the outcome may be disappointing. But for all readers unacquainted with the psychotherapeutic techniques described herein, the mystery about such matters has been demystified. The reader can try any of these procedures and decide independently the extent of the help to be derived from using them, and can also determine whether outside consultation with a certified professional is likely to be of help.

References

Alexander, F., and Ross, H. (1952). *The Impact of Freudian Psychiatry*. Chicago: The University of Chicago Press.

Dolfyn, (1987a). *Crystal Wisdom. A Beginner's Guide*. Vol. 1, rev. ed. Novato, CA: Earthspirit Inc.

_____ (1987b). *Crystal Wisdom, A Simple Advanced Guide*. Vol. 2. Novato, CA: Earthspirit Inc.

Farrow, E. P. (1945). *Analyze Yourself*. New York: International Universities Press.

Freud, S. (1949). *An Outline of Psychoanalysis*. New York: W. W. Norton.

_____ (1954). *The Origins of Psycho-Analysis, Drafts and*

Notes: 1888-1902. Ed. Marie Bonaparte, Anna Freud, Ernst Kris. New York: Basic Books.

_____ (1957). *The Standard Edition of the Complete Psychological Works of Sigmund Freud.* Vol. 14. London: The Hogarth Press.

Gottschalk, L. A. (1985). *How to Understand and Analyze Your Own Dreams.* Corona del Mar, CA: Eden Press/ Art Reproductions.

Horney, K. (1942). *Self-Analysis.* New York: W. W. Norton.

Miller, G. A. (1979). Psychology as a means of protecting human welfare. *American Psychologist* 24:1063-1075.

Pattison, M. E., Lapins, N. A., and Doerr, H. A. (1973). Faith healing. A study of personality and function. *Journal of Nervous and Mental Disease* 157: 397-409.

Pattison, M. E., and Pattison, M. L. (1980). "Ex-Gays": Religiously mediated change in homosexuals. *American Journal of Psychiatry* 137:1553-1562.

Renik, O. (1986). Countertransference in theory and practice. *Journal of the American Psychoanalytic Association* 34:699-708.

Robitscher, J. (1980). *The Powers of Psychiatry.* Boston: Houghton Mifflin.

Rosen, G. M. (1987). Self-help treatment books and the commercialization of psychotherapy. *American Psychologist* 42:46-51.

Schultz, J. H., and Luthe, W. (1969). *Autogenic Therapy.* Six volumes. New York: Grune & Stratton.

Shapiro, D. H., Jr. (1978). *Precision Nirvana.* Englewood Cliffs, NJ: Prentice-Hall.

Walsh, R. N. (1983). Meditation practice and research. *Journal of Humanistic Psychology* 23:18–50.
_____ (1984). Initial meditative experiences. In *Meditation: Classic and Contemporary Perspectives,* ed. Deane H.
Shapiro and Roger N. Walsh. Hawthorne, NY:
Aldine Publishing Co.

Index

The
Velveteen Rabbit

by Margery Williams

Illustrations by William Nicholson

CONTENTS

BOOK ONE

THE VELVETEEN RABBIT

THERE was once a velveteen rabbit, and in the beginning he was really splendid. He was fat and bunchy, as a rabbit should be; his coat was spotted brown and white, he had real thread whiskers, and his ears were lined with pink sateen. On Christmas morning, when he sat wedged in the top of the Boy's stocking, with a sprig of holly between his paws, the effect was charming.

There were other things in the stocking,

nuts and oranges and a
toy engine, and
chocolate almonds and
a clockwork mouse,
but the Rabbit was
quite the best of all.
For at least two hours
the Boy loved him, and
then Aunts and Uncles
came to dinner, and
there was a great
rustling of tissue paper
and unwrapping of

parcels, and in the excitement of looking at all the new presents the Velveteen Rabbit was forgotten.

Christmas Morning

For a long time he lived in the toy cupboard or on the nursery floor, and no one thought very much about him. He was naturally shy, and being only made of velveteen, some of the more expensive toys quite snubbed him. The mechanical toys were very superior, and looked down upon every one else; they were full of modern ideas, and pretended they were real. The model boat, who had lived through two seasons and lost most of his paint, caught the tone from them and never missed an opportunity of referring to his rigging in technical terms. The Rabbit could not claim to be a model of anything, for he didn't know that real rabbits existed; he thought they were all stuffed with sawdust like himself, and he understood that sawdust was quite out-of-date and should never be mentioned in modern circles. Even Timothy, the jointed wooden lion, who was made by the disabled soldiers, and should have had broader views, put on airs and pretended he was connected with Government. Between them all the poor little Rabbit was made to feel himself very insignificant and commonplace, and the only person who was kind to him at all was the Skin Horse.

The Skin Horse had lived longer in the nursery than any of the others. He was so old that his brown coat was bald in patches and showed the seams underneath, and most

of the hairs in his tail
had been pulled out to
string bead necklaces.
He was wise, for he
had seen a long
succession of
mechanical toys arrive
to boast and swagger,
and by-and-by break
their mainsprings and
pass away, and he knew
that they were only
toys, and would never

turn into anything else. For nursery magic is very strange and wonderful, and only those playthings that are old and wise and experienced like the Skin Horse understand all about it.

"What is REAL?" asked the Rabbit one day, when they were lying side by side near the nursery fender, before Nana came to tidy the room. "Does it mean having things that buzz inside you and a stick-out handle?"

"Real isn't how you are made," said the Skin Horse. "It's a thing that happens to you. When a child loves you for a long, long time, not

just to play with, but
REALLY loves you,
then you become
Real."

"Does it hurt?" asked
the Rabbit.

"Sometimes," said the
Skin Horse, for he was
always truthful. "When
you are Real you don't
mind being hurt."

"Does it happen all at once, like being wound up," he asked, "or bit by bit?"

"It doesn't happen all at once," said the Skin Horse. "You become. It takes a long time. That's why it doesn't happen often to people who break easily, or have sharp edges, or who have to be carefully kept. Generally, by the time you are Real, most of your hair has been loved off, and your eyes drop out and you get loose in the joints and very shabby. But these things don't matter at all, because once you are Real you can't be ugly, except to people who don't understand."

"I suppose *you* are real?" said the Rabbit. And then he wished he had not said it, for he thought the Skin Horse might be sensitive. But the Skin Horse only smiled.

The Skin Horse Tells His Story

"The Boy's Uncle made me Real," he said.

"That was a great many years ago; but once you are Real you can't become unreal again. It lasts for always."

The Rabbit sighed. He thought it would be a long time before this magic called Real happened to him. He longed to become Real, to know what it felt like; and yet the idea of growing shabby and losing his eyes and whiskers was rather sad. He wished that he could become it without these uncomfortable things happening to him.

There was a person called Nana who ruled the nursery. Sometimes she took no notice of the playthings lying

about, and sometimes,
for no reason
whatever, she went
swooping about like a
great wind and hustled
them away in
cupboards. She called
this "tidying up," and
the playthings all hated
it, especially the tin
ones. The Rabbit didn't
mind it so much, for
wherever he was

thrown he came down
soft.

One evening, when the
Boy was going to bed,
he couldn't find the
china dog that always
slept with him. Nana
was in a hurry, and it
was too much trouble
to hunt for china dogs
at bedtime, so she
simply looked about
her, and seeing that the

toy cupboard door
stood open, she made a
swoop.

"Here," she said, "take
your old Bunny! He'll
do to sleep with you!"
And she dragged the
Rabbit out by one ear,
and put him into the
Boy's arms.

That night, and for
many nights after, the

Velveteen Rabbit slept
in the Boy's bed. At
first he found it rather
uncomfortable, for the
Boy hugged him very
tight, and sometimes
he rolled over on him,
and sometimes he
pushed him so far
under the pillow that
the Rabbit could
scarcely breathe. And
he missed, too, those

long moonlight hours in the nursery, when all the house was silent, and his talks with the Skin Horse. But very soon he grew to like it, for the Boy used to talk to him, and made nice tunnels for him under the bedclothes that he said were like the burrows the real rabbits lived in. And

they had splendid
games together, in
whispers, when Nana
had gone away to her
supper and left the
night-light burning on
the mantelpiece. And
when the Boy dropped
off to sleep, the Rabbit
would snuggle down
close under his little
warm chin and dream,
with the Boy's hands

clasped close round him all night long.

And so time went on, and the little Rabbit was very happy–so happy that he never noticed how his beautiful velveteen fur was getting shabbier and shabbier, and his tail becoming unsewn, and all the pink rubbed off his nose where the Boy had kissed him.

Spring came, and they had long days in the garden, for wherever the Boy went the Rabbit went too. He had rides in the wheelbarrow, and picnics on the grass, and lovely fairy huts built for him under the raspberry canes behind the flower border. And once, when the Boy was called away suddenly to go out to tea, the Rabbit was left out on the lawn until long after dusk, and Nana had to come and look for him with the candle because the Boy couldn't go to sleep unless he was there. He was wet through with the dew and quite earthy from diving into the burrows the Boy had made for him in the flower bed, and Nana grumbled as she rubbed him off with a corner of her apron.

Spring Time

"You must have your
old Bunny!" she said.

"Fancy all that fuss for a toy!"

The Boy sat up in bed and stretched out his hands.

"Give me my Bunny!" he said. "You mustn't say that. He isn't a toy. He's REAL!"

When the little Rabbit heard that he was happy, for he knew

that what the Skin
Horse had said was
true at last. The nursery
magic had happened to
him, and he was a toy
no longer. He was Real.
The Boy himself had
said it.

That night he was
almost too happy to
sleep, and so much
love stirred in his little
sawdust heart that it

almost burst. And into
his boot-button eyes,
that had long ago lost
their polish, there came
a look of wisdom and
beauty, so that even
Nana noticed it next
morning when she
picked him up, and
said, "I declare if that
old Bunny hasn't got
quite a knowing
expression!"

That was a wonderful
Summer!

Near the house where
they lived there was a
wood, and in the long
June evenings the Boy
liked to go there after
tea to play. He took the
Velveteen Rabbit with
him, and before he
wandered off to pick
flowers, or play at

brigands among the trees, he always made the Rabbit a little nest somewhere among the bracken, where he would be quite cosy, for he was a kind-hearted little boy and he liked Bunny to be comfortable. One evening, while the Rabbit was lying there alone, watching the ants that ran to and fro between his velvet paws in the grass, he saw two strange beings creep out of the tall bracken near him.

They were rabbits like himself, but quite furry and brand-new. They must have been very well made, for their seams didn't show at all, and they changed shape in a queer way when they moved; one minute they were long and thin and the next minute fat and bunchy, instead of always staying the same like he did. Their feet padded softly on the ground, and they crept quite close to him, twitching their noses, while the Rabbit stared hard to see which side the clockwork stuck out, for he knew that people who jump generally have something to wind them up. But he couldn't see it. They were evidently a new kind of rabbit altogether.

Summer Days

They stared at him, and the little Rabbit stared back. And all the time their noses twitched.

"Why don't you get up and play with us?" one of them asked.

"I don't feel like it," said the Rabbit, for he didn't want to explain that he had no clockwork.

"Ho!" said the furry rabbit. "It's as easy as anything," And he gave a big hop sideways and stood on his hind legs.

"I don't believe you can!" he said.

"I can!" said the little Rabbit. "I can jump higher than anything!"

He meant when the Boy threw him, but of course he didn't want to say so.

"Can you hop on your hind legs?" asked the furry rabbit.

That was a dreadful question, for the Velveteen Rabbit had no hind legs at all! The back of him was made

all in one piece, like a
pincushion. He sat still
in the bracken, and
hoped that the other
rabbits wouldn't notice.

"I don't want to!" he
said again.

But the wild rabbits
have very sharp eyes.
And this one stretched
out his neck and
looked.

"He hasn't got any hind legs!" he called out. "Fancy a rabbit without any hind legs!" And he began to laugh.

"I have!" cried the little Rabbit. "I have got hind legs! I am sitting on them!"

"Then stretch them out and show me, like this!" said the wild rabbit. And he began to whirl round and dance, till the little Rabbit got quite dizzy.

"I don't like dancing," he said. "I'd rather sit still!"

But all the while he was longing to dance, for a funny new tickly feeling ran through him, and he felt he would give anything in the world to be able to jump about like these rabbits did.

The strange rabbit stopped dancing, and came quite close. He came so close this time that his long whiskers brushed the Velveteen Rabbit's ear, and then he wrinkled his nose suddenly and flattened his ears and jumped backwards.

"He doesn't smell right!" he exclaimed. "He isn't a rabbit at all! He isn't real!"

"I *am* Real!" said the little Rabbit. "I am Real! The Boy said so!" And he nearly began to cry.

Just then there was a sound of footsteps, and the Boy ran past near them, and with a stamp of feet and a flash of white tails the two strange rabbits disappeared.

"Come back and play with me!" called the little Rabbit. "Oh, do come back! I *know* I am Real!"

But there was no answer, only the little ants ran to and fro, and the bracken swayed gently where the two strangers had passed. The Velveteen Rabbit was all alone.

"Oh, dear!" he thought. "Why did they run away like that? Why couldn't they stop and talk to me?"

For a long time he lay very still, watching the bracken, and hoping that they would come back. But they never returned, and presently the sun sank lower and the little white moths fluttered out, and the Boy came and carried him home.

Weeks passed, and the little Rabbit grew very old and shabby, but the Boy loved him just as much. He loved him so hard that he loved all his whiskers off, and the pink lining to his ears turned grey, and his brown spots faded. He even began to lose his shape, and he scarcely looked like a rabbit any more, except to the Boy. To him he was always beautiful, and that was all that the little Rabbit cared about. He didn't mind how he looked to other people, because the nursery magic had made him Real, and when you are Real shabbiness doesn't matter.

And then, one day, the Boy was ill.

His face grew very flushed, and he talked in his sleep, and his little body was so hot that it burned the Rabbit when he held him close. Strange people came and went in the nursery, and a light burned all night and through it all the

little Velveteen Rabbit
lay there, hidden from
sight under the
bedclothes, and he
never stirred, for he
was afraid that if they
found him some one
might take him away,
and he knew that the
Boy needed him.

It was a long weary
time, for the Boy was
too ill to play, and the

little Rabbit found it rather dull with nothing to do all day long. But he snuggled down patiently, and looked forward to the time when the Boy should be well again, and they would go out in the garden amongst the flowers and the butterflies and play splendid games in the raspberry thicket like they used to. All sorts of delightful things he planned, and while the Boy lay half asleep he crept up close to the pillow and whispered them in his ear. And presently the fever turned, and the Boy got better. He was able to sit up in bed and look at picture-books, while

the little Rabbit
cuddled close at his
side. And one day, they
let him get up and
dress.

It was a bright, sunny
morning, and the
windows stood wide
open. They had carried
the Boy out on to the
balcony, wrapped in a
shawl, and the little
Rabbit lay tangled up

among the bedclothes, thinking.

The Boy was going to the seaside to-morrow. Everything was arranged, and now it only remained to carry out the doctor's orders. They talked about it all, while the little Rabbit lay under the bedclothes, with just his head peeping out, and listened. The room was to be disinfected, and all the books and toys that the Boy had played with in bed must be burnt.

"Hurrah!" thought the little Rabbit. "To-morrow we shall go to the seaside!" For the boy had often talked of the seaside, and he wanted very much to

see the big waves
coming in, and the tiny
crabs, and the sand
castles.

Just then Nana caught
sight of him.

"How about his old
Bunny?" she asked.

"*That?*" said the doctor.
"Why, it's a mass of
scarlet fever germs!—
Burn it at once. What?

Nonsense! Get him a new one. He mustn't have that any more!"

Anxious Times

And so the little Rabbit was put into a sack

with the old picture-
books and a lot of
rubbish, and carried
out to the end of the
garden behind the
fowl-house. That was a
fine place to make a
bonfire, only the
gardener was too busy
just then to attend to it.
He had the potatoes to
dig and the green peas
to gather, but next

morning he promised to come quite early and burn the whole lot.

That night the Boy slept in a different bedroom, and he had a new bunny to sleep with him. It was a splendid bunny, all white plush with real glass eyes, but the Boy was too excited to care very much about it. For

to-morrow he was
going to the seaside,
and that in itself was
such a wonderful thing
that he could think of
nothing else.

And while the Boy was
asleep, dreaming of the
seaside, the little Rabbit
lay among the old
picture-books in the
corner behind the
fowl-house, and he felt

very lonely. The sack
had been left untied,
and so by wriggling a
bit he was able to get
his head through the
opening and look out.
He was shivering a
little, for he had always
been used to sleeping
in a proper bed, and by
this time his coat had
worn so thin and
threadbare from

hugging that it was no longer any protection to him. Near by he could see the thicket of raspberry canes, growing tall and close like a tropical jungle, in whose shadow he had played with the Boy on bygone mornings. He thought of those long sunlit hours in the garden—how happy

they were—and a great
sadness came over him.
He seemed to see them
all pass before him,
each more beautiful
than the other, the fairy
huts in the flower-bed,
the quiet evenings in
the wood when he lay
in the bracken and the
little ants ran over his
paws; the wonderful
day when he first knew

that he was Real. He thought of the Skin Horse, so wise and gentle, and all that he had told him. Of what use was it to be loved and lose one's beauty and become Real if it all ended like this? And a tear, a real tear, trickled down his little shabby velvet nose and fell to the ground.

And then a strange thing happened. For where the tear had fallen a flower grew out of the ground, a mysterious flower, not at all like any that grew in the garden. It had slender green leaves the colour of emeralds, and in the centre of the leaves a blossom like a golden cup. It was so beautiful that the little Rabbit forgot to cry, and just lay there watching it. And presently the blossom opened, and out of it there stepped a fairy.

She was quite the loveliest fairy in the whole world. Her dress was of pearl and dew-drops, and there were flowers round her neck and in her hair, and her face was like the most perfect flower of all. And she came close to the little Rabbit and gathered him up in her arms and kissed him on his velveteen nose that was all damp from crying.

"Little Rabbit," she said, "don't you know who I am?"

The Rabbit looked up at her, and it seemed to him that he had seen her face before, but he couldn't think where.

"I am the nursery magic Fairy," she said. "I take care of all the playthings that the children have loved. When they are old and worn out and the children don't need them any more, then I come and take them away with me and turn them into Real."

"Wasn't I Real before?" asked the little Rabbit.

"You were Real to the Boy," the Fairy said, "because he loved you. Now you shall be Real to every one."

The Fairy Flower

And she held the little Rabbit close in her

arms and flew with him into the wood.

It was light now, for the moon had risen. All the forest was beautiful, and the fronds of the bracken shone like frosted silver. In the open glade between the tree-trunks the wild rabbits danced with their shadows on the velvet grass, but when they saw the Fairy they all stopped dancing and stood round in a ring to stare at her.

"I've brought you a new playfellow," the Fairy said. "You must be very kind to him and teach him all he needs to know in Rabbit-land, for he is going to live with you for ever and ever!"

And she kissed the little Rabbit again and put him down on the grass.

"Run and play, little Rabbit!" she said.

But the little Rabbit sat quite still for a moment and never moved. For when he saw all the wild rabbits dancing around him he suddenly remembered about his hind legs, and he didn't want them to see that he was made all in one piece. He did not know that when the Fairy kissed him that last time she had changed him altogether. And he might have sat there a

long time, too shy to
move, if just then
something hadn't
tickled his nose, and
before he thought what
he was doing he lifted
his hind toe to scratch
it.

And he found that he
actually had hind legs!
Instead of dingy
velveteen he had
brown fur, soft and

shiny, his ears twitched by themselves, and his whiskers were so long that they brushed the grass. He gave one leap and the joy of using those hind legs was so great that he went springing about the turf on them, jumping sideways and whirling round as the others did, and he grew so

excited that when at
last he did stop to look
for the Fairy she had
gone.

He was a Real Rabbit
at last, at home with
the other rabbits.

At Last! At Last!

Autumn passed and Winter, and in the Spring, when the days grew warm and sunny, the Boy went out to play in the wood behind the house. And while he was playing, two rabbits crept out from the bracken and peeped at him. One of them was brown all over, but the other had strange markings under his fur, as though long ago he had been spotted, and the spots still showed through. And about his little soft nose and his round black eyes there was something familiar, so that the Boy thought to himself:

"Why, he looks just like my old Bunny that was

lost when I had scarlet fever!"

But he never knew that it really was his own Bunny, come back to look at the child who had first helped him to be Real.

BOOK TWO

COLORING BOOKS FOR KIDS

Made in the USA
Columbia, SC
22 February 2021